Photography by Ray Main

suzanne davy

101 IDEAS
bedrooms

BARNES
& NOBLE
BOOKS
NEW YORK

This edition published by Barnes & Noble,
Inc. by arrangement with Quadrille
Publishing Ltd.

2004 Barnes & Noble books

M 10 9 8 7 6 5 4 3 2 1

ISBN 0-7607-6145-0

Editorial Director Jane O'Shea
Art Director Helen Lewis
Designer Paul Welti
Project Editor Hilary Mandleberg
Production Beverley Richardson

Photography Ray Main

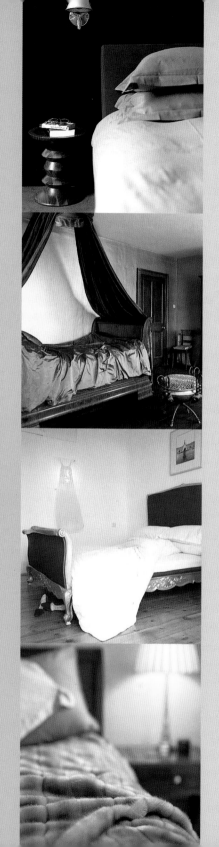

contents

part one
the big picture

part one

the big picture

where do I start?
five things to do before you begin

Designing your bedroom should be a creative and satisfying business, but to keep the project on track, a degree of practicality is essential as a starting point.

jottings

Small practical procedures will make a big difference to your organizational process! Arm yourself with a pen and notebook, because you'll find inspiration all around you and will need to jot down sources, references, and ideas.

money, measure, and management

You'll find a calculator, long tape measure, and color-coded files or folders essential. Shoe boxes might come in handy for storing inspirational finds. Also, tags, tape, light glue, paper clips, and pins.

inspirational stuff

Be like a squirrel and hoard magazines, brochures, and color charts. The back pages of interior design magazines are a rich source for manufacturers' brochures. At this stage just have fun exploring your intuitive awareness of styles, colors, and shapes.

stripping

Thinking about how your bedroom will look naked will help you make a critical appraisal; you'll find that the room's architecture, natural light, and spatial potential will be revealed (see 3). An undressed bedroom may also suggest a more thorough decorating program than you had envisaged!

questions, questions

Write down questions as and when they arise. You don't have to answer them all yet, but they will help your scheme evolve. Your list of questions—and answers—will grow as your plan develops. For example, are there any basic priorities such as re-wiring and (if adding a bath) plumbing? Do I have to compromise with existing decorations and furnishings? Where do I go for inspiration?

make a wish list

A wish list is a useful exercise to help you prioritize what you want to achieve in your bedroom. Obviously, if there are two of you, it's essential to explore and express your individual likes and dislikes— and probably find compromise on the way!

overall benefits
- I want a bedroom that will add to the value of my house
- I want to maximize the space
- I want a quick, cheap update
- I want to get away from street noise and pollution

function
- I want a sexy bedroom
- I want a quiet haven that I can retreat to
- I want a room where I can work sometimes
- I want a room where I can listen to my music
- I want a room where I can bathe
- I want a room to put up a guest
- I want somewhere to display my picture collection

built-ins
- I need generous closet space
- I want a hideaway office
- I need lots of bookshelves
- I want a way to zone the bed area

details
- I want a hardwood floor
- I want to include underfloor heating
- I want a huge modern bed
- I want better lighting and heating

what are my assets? 3

Every bedroom has potential, however forlorn it might appear at the outset, so find ways of highlighting its merits.

space
• Create an en-suite bathroom or an in-room bathing area
• Increase your storage or closet space
• Buy a new big bed
• In a high-ceilinged room, take advantage and install a mezzanine or bed platform

good natural light
• Make the most of it—don't block it with heavy draperies
• Choose colors to maximize its effect

architectural detail
• Moldings, old-fashioned windows, old fireplaces, and paneled doors all add character and decorating potential

floor
• Old floorboards don't have to be covered (see 71)
• A carpet in good condition will be kind to your budget

furniture and ornament
• If you already have good storage space, lucky you!
• A special piece of furniture you possess may influence your decorative direction
• A dynamic painting or picture can be the starting point for your color theme (see 96)

dump the lame ducks 4

Now is the time to take stock. Update or renovate where you can, but don't jeopardize your new bedroom by hanging on to things.

flooring
Flooring is not the place to compromise (see 76–81). If your old carpeting is beyond hope, or is highly colored or patterned, get rid of it rather than ruin the harmony of your new plan.

bedroom furniture
If your bed has started to sag or squeak, it's time to buy a new one (see 78–80). This is also the moment to get rid of any cheaply made built-in furniture and go for some updated storage instead (see 85).

wires and pipes
There will never be a better opportunity to get rid of visible pipes and dangling electric light cords.

lighting
If all you have is a central ceiling light in your bedroom, it's likely that it'll provide only unflattering illumination. If you can, replace it with downlights, wall, and table lamps; if you can't, a dimmer switch might help (see 53–56).

top tips for tiny bedrooms

5

Making the most of a tiny space involves crafty use of space, color, lighting, and furnishings.

shape and line

Keep the decorative theme simple, and make the bed the focus, preferably positioning it opposite the door to draw the eye. An oversized object, such as a very large picture behind the bed, can give the illusion of space. Vertical or horizontal lines or stripes visually accentuate height or length respectively, but dominating pattern or shape elsewhere will counteract the effect.

color

Cool colors such as light greens and blues recede, creating a sense of space. A hint of yellow in the green or red in the blue helps to avoid a "cold" atmosphere, while using a darker "anchor" color prevents pale colors from looking insipid and gives definition. A ceiling in a pale, neutral color—preferably not pure white—with a slight sheen will reflect and enhance natural light.

lighting

An uncluttered window maximizes natural light—choose blinds, shades or shutters, rather than draperies. Balanced electric lighting around the room prevents shadowy corners, and walls can be "extended" with uplights. Slender, elongated lamps and shades accentuate height, while wall- or bed-mounted reading lights save space. Be careful when using spotlights, as they are inclined to create harsh pools of light and upset the decorative rhythm.

mirrors

Mirrors maximize light, but a large area of them can create glare and be unnerving. Instead, use mirror in panels—for example, on the front of closet doors or either side of the bed.

furniture and storage

Small furniture won't make the room look bigger; it's better to have fewer good-sized pieces. Dual-purpose storage saves space: A bed with drawers underneath, a window seat, a blanket chest bedside table, even a fold-down vanity table in a closet to keep clutter to a minimum. If possible, have sliding doors on closets, and replace protruding handles with flush ones or touch-opening magnets, as appropriate.

under the rafters

There's something very appealing about sleeping under the rafters, but only when there's enough room to stand up straight when you get out of bed! The inherent quirkiness of the space lends it great character, and this can be exploited to create a uniquely attractive environment. But any conversion will require the expertise of an architect, surveyor, or building contractor who will offer guidance on building regulations and structural requirements.

fitting furniture

Furniture in attic rooms needs to be low and streamlined, but this means problematic clothes storage. You could build a false wall "hung" from the ceiling, but this will upset the symmetry of the space. A more radical solution is a freestanding closet and drawer unit. One side gives access to your clothes, and the other can be your "headboard."

bed placement

The bed has to be positioned so that you don't hit your head every time you sit up. Apart from the freestanding unit option, the obvious solution is to put the bed against the gable wall, though if there's a window in this, you may not have room for a headboard. In this case, have an oversized headboard, and turn the bed around to face the window.

making it special

There is little opportunity in an attic bedroom to use fabrics, wallcoverings, pictures, or other ornamentation, so focus on the room's interesting lines and features instead. If there's a lot of floor, exploit it with a wood or laminate floor. With low ceilings, clever lighting—floor lighting, for example—can help avoid any sense of claustrophobia, and if there's plenty of space, think about incorporating a toilet and shower behind a false wall.

advantages of creating an attic bedroom

- Adds value to the house
- Makes use of wasted space
- Appealing character
- Removed from the main hubbub of the house
- The space can be larger than any other room in the house
- The view may be great

disadvantages of creating an attic bedroom

- Cost
- Intrusiveness of access stairs
- Difficult to get correct balance of light and heat
- Arrangement of furniture can be awkward
- Difficult access for large furniture
- Loss of storage space

7 children's rooms

A child's room needs to grow with the child. Starting off as a quiet, warm place for baby to sleep, it will soon become a playground, study area, sports hall, den, and/or karaoke club.

space-saving sleeping

At the toddler stage, a bed built into a wall unit or a low platform bed are good choices. A more dramatic option is to construct a low mezzanine with the bed up a short flight of stairs and a study and play area beneath.

furniture

Avoid kids' furniture; instead, choose a good shelving system and adaptable furniture. A couple of low chests of drawers with laminated boards on top offer storage space, a hideaway den, and, later, a desk.

storage

Use color-coded boxes or baskets for larger toys and hanging drawstring bags for smaller items. Store books in a basket or on a low shelf, but keep special books on higher shelves, out of the reach of sticky fingers.

windows

Windows must have safety catches and/or locks that can be opened easily in case of fire.

flooring

Go for easy-care flooring like rubber, floorboards, or laminate (see 66, 67), but for the crawling and learning-to-walk stage, a large area rug will make life's ups and downs easier.

lighting

All electrical outlets must be childproof. For children who are afraid of the dark, dimmer switches and low-wattage baseboard nightlights are discreet. Older children need task lighting for study, hobbies, and reading in bed.

decoration

A child's tastes and interests change, so use easy-to-alter paint rather than wallpaper. Other details such as curtains, bed linen, lampshades, and cushions can be updated without too much trouble and expense.

8 do I need a professional?

If your bedroom and (possibly) en-suite bath project involves work that you can't do yourself, you will need some professional input. This list will help you identify the kinds of people you may have to call on and explains what they do.

architect

- Converts your ideas into reality
- Provides working drawings; deals with building codes
- Conservation and restoration
- Construction techniques
- Project management
- Special requirements, such as air-conditioning or en-suite bathroom design

lighting consultant

- Specialist in lighting design, using the latest technology and effects

building contractor

- Remodeling
- Removing or constructing partition walls
- Stripping walls, plastering, and finishing
- Installing doors and windows
- General electric and plumbing work
- Hard flooring and general carpentry
- General painting and decorating, and tiling

carpenter

- Built-in closets and complex shelving
- Bed platforms
- Cornice board and headboard cutouts
- Window frame and door resizing and hanging
- Renovation of wooden floors

plumber

- Bathroom and toilet installation
- Water and heating expertise

electrician

- Advice on wiring safety compliance
- Planning and installation of outlets, switches, and lighting
- Rewiring

interior designer

- Stylistic guidance
- Descriptive drawings
- Access to a wide range of samples
- Advice on lighting and ornamentation

- A link between architect and client
- Knowledge of special finishes, paint effects, carpets, fabrics, and materials

upholsterer and curtain/drapery maker

- Headboard and bed hangings
- Made-to-order bolsters and cushions
- Slipcovers
- Making and hanging curtains, draperies, and shades

9 set a budget

First decide whether you are going to pay for the whole job on completion, stagger the work and the payment, or borrow to fund your bedroom makeover. Once you've decided how much you are able to spend, put aside 10% of the total for the inevitable unforeseen contingencies. Keep in mind that your outlay will relate to whether you want to add capital value to the property or whether you are just doing an economic makeover. You will need to allocate your budget proportionally, depending on the relative expense of each part of the work. For example:

- General building costs
- New en-suite bathroom
- Rewiring
- Painting and decorating
- Flooring, fixtures, and fittings, including bed and carpentry
- Fabrics and making costs
- Professional fees (see 10)

If you go over your budget, don't panic (see 11).

10 cost it out

Make three lists to help you draw up your budget. The first sets out the major work, including structural alterations, electricity and plumbing, en-suite bathroom upgrading or installation, carpentry, and flooring. Don't forget to budget for any professional help.

The second list costs out wallpaper and papering, paint and painting, bed, fabric, furniture, window treatment, storage, light fixtures, audio, and TV system. Again, factor in professional help with these components.

The third list includes all the accessories that you have to buy new (well, retail therapy is vital!) such as bed linen, pillows, cushions, throws, rugs, mirrors, and decorative objects.

Try to be realistic about what you can afford, remembering to keep 10% for contingencies. Always keep necessity, quality, and comfort in mind when you define your priorities!

11
small budget—big ideas five
ways to make your money go further

If you've got lots of ideas but little cash, you have several options: doing it yourself, phasing the work, or exploring some cost-cutting ideas.

1 • doing your own thing

Your three-part list (see 10) will help you identify which sections of your bedroom project you can tackle yourself. Don't be overambitious, though, because you could waste time, energy, and, ultimately, money. However, doing all the painting and wallpapering, and painting any newly made storage furniture, for example, will save you a lot of money.

2 • phasing the work

See if your budget will cover your absolute priorities such as rewiring and plumbing, a new bed or an en-suite shower, for example. Another option is to install the plumbing up to "first fit" — in other words, putting in the pipework only and installing the fixtures at a later date, when you have more funds.

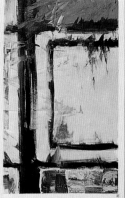

3 • paint it on

Paint is less expensive than wallpaper, and painting saves time and effort as well. It's also more versatile because of its range of colors and finishes, and if you make a bad choice, you can always try again.

4 • material world

You can save money on fabric by using cheaper materials, but in generous quantities, for curtains, draperies, and bed dressing. For example, use dress-weight silk instead of furnishing-weight, muslin instead of voile, cotton instead of linen. Instead of draperies, you might like to make a feature out of a home-painted roller shade.

5 • feature focus

Go for chic minimalism with maximum effect by making a stunning feature of one piece of furniture—probably the bed—and focus maximum attention on that area. This will set the tone for your high standards and the future direction of the design when money allows.

12

bedroom upgrade

Instead of going for a complete redesign, it's easy enough to change the look of your bedroom by concentrating on one or two major features, or by going for some quick decorative fixes.

three major options

1 • Floor: Since flooring is crucial, a new-look floor will go a long way to rejuvenating the room. To upgrade existing floorboards, sand, fill, and finish them appropriately; or, if they can't be satisfactorily repaired, you might paint a broad border around the perimeter and cover the rest of the floor with a large rug. If this process is too laborious, carpeting may be preferable.

2 • Window: If you have only had blinds or shades before, adding curtains or draperies will change the visual emphasis of the bedroom. Professionally made draperies add substance and drama.

3 • Bed: Expense, rather than time and effort, will get you a beautiful new bed in a style that could suggest a new decorative direction for you to follow.

five quick fixes

1 • Walls: Color refreshes the decorative emphasis, and paint is the easiest and cheapest way to achieve this. Alternatively, change the look from solid-colored to patterned with wallpaper; or, for a fresh and opulent look, line the entire wall behind the bed with a fabric such as felt or damask.

2 • Ceiling: Painting the ceiling a contrasting color will change the room's visual dynamic.

3 • Window: Replace a dated window treatment with a simple modern blind, shade shutters, or sheer curtain. If you have treasured curtains or draperies, give them new life with a broad fabric border.

4 • Bed: New bed dressing will immediately refresh your bedroom look. Change the color and texture by using contrasting fabrics (see 44) while keeping in touch with the room's overall style. Replace a tired headboard with panels of material, or simply hang a large painting over the bed.

5 • Doors and drawers: Repaint storage units and modernize them with new door handles for both a visual and a tactile makeover.

13 blow-the-budget bedrooms

Here are some tempting ideas for delicious extravagance that you might be able to fit into your budget.

sizing up

Why be content with the existing dimensions of your bedroom? If you can sacrifice an adjoining room, knock through and claim it, either as an en-suite bathroom or as a dressing room/bathroom zone.

bathing in luxury

Indulge in a spa bath with a separate multi-jet shower and aromatherapy steam fixture. If space is limited, a Japanese-style square wooden bathtub is a sleek alternative (see 17 and 33).

underfoot

How about wall-to-wall carpeting with a contrasting border (see 68) or a contemporary rug in a design to suit your style (see 69)? And while you are at it, underfloor heating is not impossibly expensive (see 16 and 66).

fantasy bed

Get the best-quality bed you can and the largest that will happily fit in the room.

light and sound

A professionally designed lighting system is worth the expense, and since rewiring is involved anyway, why not add a state-of-the-art TV and audio system, too (see 18 and 91)?

carpentry

Custom-made carpentry gives you storage that exactly suits your needs and bedroom style (see 85).

luxurious fabrics

Indulge in luxurious fabrics like pure silk, velvet, cashmere, mohair, faux fur, suede, or leather (see 44 and 48). There are so many places and ways to use them in a bedroom.

custom-made creations

Hand-finished draperies are a supreme indulgence; tailored upholstery on a chair or stool looks sophisticated; and for a luxurious extra, commission hand-made cushions and bolsters.

14
upscale materials

Introducing top-quality materials will elevate any decorative theme, even if they're used economically.

fabric

Cashmere, mohair, faux fur, and velvet for throws and cushions and silk for draperies look sumptuous. Consider different fabrics for everything from walls to draperies, chairs to bedspreads.

bedding

The finest sheets are Egyptian cotton and Irish linen—costly and high-maintenance, but definitely worth it.

pillows

Lots of plump pillows provide a stylish finish for the well-dressed bed. The softest and most luxurious filling is goose down.

carpet

All-wool carpets are the best you can buy; or you could indulge in a fun but luxurious-looking deep shag-pile rug (see 68, 69).

wooden floor

Unusual woods for a floor are brandy-toned Kempas, pink-tinged Rose Gum Eucalyptus, and tea-colored Merbau.

leather

The utlimate luxury is leather—tiles and hides for flooring, walls, furniture, paneling, and head- and footboards, or suede for walls and upholstery.

wallpaper

Handpainted and made-to-order papers are expensive, but just a panel or two will look stunning.

paint

Suede-effect paint is not expensive but looks luxurious. High-gloss paints that imitate lacquer can be used on plaster, wood, and metal.

glass

Mirrored and glass furniture is making a big comeback. Just one item will add "edge" to a scheme.

marble

Marble has always embodied luxury. Choose from highly polished classical marble and "tumbled" finishes with a tactile, earthy appearance.

make a plan

A scale plan is an absolute necessity. It will be your blueprint for all stages, from planning electrical and plumbing work to estimating paint or wallpaper quantities and placing TV and audio systems.

Using graph or quadrille paper, draw to scale the room's dimensions, doors, windows, radiators, outlets, switches, and so on, and make to-scale templates of furniture to see how it will fit in. When your plan is finished, give a copy of it to any contractors.

It's also useful to have a plan of each wall, showing doors, windows, baseboards, alcoves, light switches, and wall plugs. This will help you estimate paint, wallpaper, and window fabric, quantities and shelving, and storage requirements. Architectural details, such as cornices, paneling, and baseboards, give you a working template for painting.

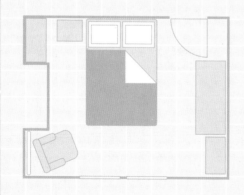

heating and ventilation

A comfortable bedroom temperature is 73°F and a bathroom 65°F. Ventilation should provide fresh air and control humidity and should be as silent and discreet as possible.

radiators

If you have radiators rather than baseboard heat or forced-air heating/cooling, fear not. Radiators are now an acceptable part of an interior. Modern ones come in all shapes and in finishes, from matte black to brilliant chrome. Retro-style radiators suit robust contemporary interiors. If you choose restored radiators, make sure they have been correctly adapted for modern plumbing.

A radiator is often sited under a window, but if you have long curtains or draperies, you may want to locate it on an interior wall instead. If you dislike the look of a radiator, simply camouflage it with paint to match the wall.

underfloor heating

Most underfloor (or infloor) heating is installed at the building stage, but there are systems that can be laid in isolation, which makes them an option for a new en-suite bath. There are two types of underfloor heating. A hot-water system runs through flexible pipes, while an electric one uses wires or matting. Some systems can be integrated with radiators, and certain types can be used with marble, ceramic, stone, vinyl, wood, and even carpet.

ventilation

Air-conditioning works well, has flexible temperature control, and reduces interior pollution and allergens. Although a ceiling fan doesn't have air-changing qualities, it produces a cool breeze.

humidity

An insulated and air-conditioned environment can be dehydrating. Resolve the problem by having a bowl of water in the room and renewing the water every day. A dehumidifier is a high-tech option!

bath

A bathroom or shower room needs instant heating and ventilation. If you need to install a new radiator in the bath, you might consider a towel-warming rail—the kind that doubles as a radiator while keeping towels deliciously warm. An extractor fan is vital.

17
plumbing and electricity

- Have your plan at hand when you consult the electrician and plumber, so you can discuss any structural changes and make sure the jobs are carried out in the right order (see 21).
- Having plenty of electrical outlets—inside closets, too—avoids unsightly outlet strips and extensions.
- Consider having air-conditioning or at least a ceiling fan.
- Make a list of what you need to do and obtain: electricity outlets, lights, air-conditioning, ceiling fan, ventilation, plumbing for a bath, if any.
- Never attempt to deal with electricity yourself when it comes anywhere near the "wet" elements of your project!

18
audio and television

A good sound and vision system in the bedroom is a luxury, but once you've got one, you won't look back.

- Make sure you coordinate the installation with your other building and decorating works (see 21).
- For comfortable TV viewing a 12-inch screen at the end of the bed is adequate, but if the TV is farther away, you will probably want a 22-inch screen.
- For the best acoustics, have the audio speakers facing something soft—such as the bed.
- We generally watch TV and listen to music at a lower volume in the bedroom, so you probably won't need big speakers.
- If you are adding an en-suite bath, you might want to install a special audio speaker designed for bathroom use.
- If your system doesn't merit being part of the decorative design, build it all into a customized cabinet.
- The simplest audio system for a bedroom is a compact, wall-mounted system.

19 safety matters

More "home time" hours are spent in the bedroom than in any other room in the house. Minimizing the risks from fire, flood, electrical faults, and middle-of the-night trips to the bathroom will allow you to sleep in peace.

- Fabrics and bedding materials should be fire retardant and comply with safety standards
- Have fire extinguishers on hand, both during and after construction work
- Never leave candles lit at night or if you are out of the room
- Install smoke alarms
- Make sure you have a safety escape and that everyone knows how to use it
- Provide a plug-in "nightlight" for children and guests
- Never use electrical appliances near water
- Light switches, fixtures, and shaving outlets in the bathroom must comply with safety codes
- Make sure all windows have a locking system and a key that is accessible
- Closet doors in children's rooms should have safety catches or childproof catches where necessary
- Regularly check that bunk ladders are stable
- Take care on stepladders when you are accessing high-level storage space
- Use low-odor paints if possible
- Static electricity in synthetic materials such as some nylon carpets is considered to be harmful by some people
- Electrical appliances emit radiation and electromagnetic fields unless they are turned off at source

20 finding the right people to help

Creating the bedroom of your dreams is a huge undertaking. Professional help is invaluable, both at the planning/designing stage and for the work itself.

architect

Use a certified architect who will know local contractors. You are not obligated to have the architect find the contractor. Architects charge a percentage or an hourly rate, but you might be able to negotiate an all-inclusive price. Expect to be invoiced at stages during the work.

building contractor

Use a local firm, and go by personal recommendation: What were they like to work with? Were they on schedule and within budget? Check on their standard of work via their professional association and to confirm that they are financially stable. A smart letterhead isn't proof. For a big project especially, you might want to check if their professional association has a guarantee program against the firm going out of business. Better safe than very sorry! Always seek alternative estimates for comparison.

a bad contractor:

- Won't produce properly written quotations
- Won't have a registered business address
- Won't be able to offer good references
- May not carry the right kind of insurance
- May be unwilling to sign any sort of contract
- Is unlikely to employ properly trained labor
- Will be unwilling to redress complaints
- Will work short hours; may not appear at all
- Doesn't like to clean up!

plumber, electrician, and carpenter

Find either by word of mouth or through your contractor. Check references and employ only a fully qualified and registered plumber or electrician.

interior designer

Find a local one either by recommendation or through their store; or you may find one from having seen their work in a book, magazine article, or advertisement. It's usual to pay travel expenses, a daily rate, and a percentage mark-up on furnishings that they've sourced.

soft furnishings maker

Find a soft furnishings maker, drapery maker, or upholsterer either by word of mouth, through retail furniture or fabric outlets, or in a large department store with its own design service.

order of work

Having an understanding of the order in which work should be completed will help your budgeting and time management, as well as providing a template for the contractors so the project can proceed with seamless efficiency!

structure

- Remove or alter partition walls; erect new ones
- Install new services to "first fit" (pipes and wires for electricity, telephone, TV, audio, plumbing, central heating, underfloor heating, and electric ventilation)
- Strip old wallpaper and repair plaster
- Lay hard flooring
- Repair or install baseboards and cornices
- Hang new doors and repair or replace window frames and windows
- Install built-in furniture, bed platform, window seats, and so on
- "Second fit": Install and connect radiators, sinks, bathtub; fix electricity outlets and light fixtures
- Affix tiles

decorating

- Apply undercoat and first coat of paint or line walls and ceiling. This may be done before "second fit" to prevent naked spots behind radiators
- Apply final paint finish or hang wallpaper
- Lay carpet
- Install fixed shelving
- Attach curtain/drapery hardware
- Hang window treatments
- Attach light fixtures
- Position bed and furniture
- Add pictures, mirrors, and ornaments

part two

getting down to the detail

22 find your look

Creating an inspiration or mood board gives you the opportunity to put together an assortment of decorating materials and stimuli that will help you identify and develop your decorating style.

Take two large sheets of black or dark gray cardboard (a dark background "frames" the materials well). On the first, stick, clip, or pin intuitive choices taken from your hoard of paint charts, magazines, catalogs, and so on. Build on this with ephemeral inspirations, i.e. things you like for their texture or mood but that aren't to be used themselves—a feather, perhaps, or a tortoiseshell button, a scrap of antique material, or a leaf skeleton. You could photograph any items that can't be attached to the board. Analyzing why you respond positively to each element will help you find the mood of the design. In this way the foundation of your decorative plan will emerge.

The second board brings the design into focus with real samples and with photographs of hard ingredients, such as radiators, light fixtures, and storage units. Deal with the main elements first: paint color, wall and floor coverings, major fabrics, and bathroom surfaces, if relevant. Include lots of alternatives so you can mix and match and keep your options open as the plan comes together. Buy large samples that show the whole pattern repeat and cut them to size according to their proportional use in the bedroom. Observe how color, pattern, and texture relate to each other and to all the other elements such as flooring, furniture, and lighting effects. It's a good idea to experiment with paint colors on large pieces of paper and hang them in the bedroom to see how the space and light affects them. An important observation is to see how your chosen colors, patterns, and textures look in daylight, electric light, or candlelight.

23 modern comfort

Here quality prevails and no single element dominates. Furniture is comfortable, there is plenty of storage and sumptuous fabrics, and textures achieve a dressed-up effect.

colors

Choose a couple of understated but not monochrome colors and one highlight, such as
- Caramel, cream, and pistachio
- Silver gray, mole, plum
- Ground ginger, chalk, and sapphire

bed

A modern four-poster gives scope for lavish bed dressing. Top with an oversized headboard upholstered in a textured fabric.

walls

In a large room, use pattern—a strongly patterned wallpaper on one wall—or contrasting color to break up the wall surface. Alternatively, matte and satin-finish paints in the same color on different walls look subtle.

window

Generous draperies—perhaps silk mix for outer draperies and linen for the inner, edged in a contrasting fabric—with simple headings.

flooring

Velvety carpeting, such as cut-pile wool or wool-blend (see 67), is a must. For pattern, consider modern carpeting with subtle color and a quiet design.

lighting

Thoughtful details—reading lights at just the right height, dimmer switches, and accent lights—add the finishing touch.

furniture

Upholstery should be simple and good-looking, with the focus on comfort, finish, and texture. A chaise longue or easy chair and a dressing table are perfect, while the ideal storage would be a walk-in closet with his and her compartments!

accessories

Boldness is key—a single beautiful mirror or painting, groups of smaller pictures, and one or two oversized ornaments to anchor the whole.

24 minimalist

A haven of harmony and spaciousness using selective ingredients that are adaptable, comfortable, and full of character. If you're able to live with limited furniture and decoration, or you're on a tight budget, the minimalist look is for you.

colors

Go for a very pure monotone palette, allowing shape and texture to add interest, or use some color to compensate for minimal furnishing and decoration. Strong, but not loud, color can be used in a controlled way, so harmony is maintained in your palette:

• Chalk white, stone, bone, coffee
• Willow-pattern blue, antique silver, and chalk
• Moss green, stone, and lime white

walls

Use your strong color with discretion, perhaps on the bed wall only, to emphasize that area. Paint is preferable to wallpaper, but you can introduce different paint finishes, such as subtle horizontal stripes of matte and satin. Choose a neutral background shade where you aren't using color.

window

You could paint the unadorned window and window frame in an accent color and fit a simple shade or install slatted shutters.

bed

Sleek and low lines with simple bedding that echoes the color theme. Texture is essential, but two contrasts are enough. Alternatively, make the bed the center of attention: use a beautiful antique carved bed perhaps, or a stylish four-poster.

floor

Bare floorboards are the obvious foundation for the minimalist look. They could be stripped and sealed or given a white colorwash. Rubber tiles, cork, or unglazed tiles would be appropriate, too.

lighting

Good lighting is essential, but it doesn't have to be sophisticated. Illuminate the four corners of the room with floor-mounted uplights to maximize the sense of space, and use simple, sleek lamps for task and mood lighting. If you have a single special decorative item, spotlight it for impact.

storage

Maximizing storage will eliminate clutter, so long as it's easily usable with generous space, so that things can be put away without fuss. You could even raise the bed on a box platform with built-in drawers underneath.

furniture

One special piece of furniture will set off the look and make a greater contribution than three mundane items! Think of shape and color, no matter whether the piece is modern or a battered antique.

accessories

Pictures look great in uniform frames hung in a geometric block. Add a large mirror with a broad frame to accentuate the feeling of spaciousness, and spotlight a single, spectacular flower in a brightly colored vase.

25 zen zone

Western comfort and convenience infuse the serenity of a traditional Japanese sleeping zone. There is emphasis on surfaces; natural materials feature above color; and refined shape and line create harmony and space.

colors

Indigo blue is traditionally the key color, with other color coming from natural materials and black and white highlights. Choose additional colors, like jade green, to promote serenity.
- Indigo blue, porcelain white, bamboo
- Rice white, ebony, maple
- Jade green, ivory, gray, black lacquer

window

Simple white shades or blinds are best or, for texture, grass fiber, matchstick (see 71), or bamboo. Translucent paper screens provide privacy but filter the light.

bed

Replace the traditional futon on tatami mats with a plain blond-wood bed on low legs or "floating" on a base, or with a sleeping platform enclosed by sliding screens. Dress the bed with bolsters and plain bed coverings.

walls

Emphasizing space and light is essential to the Zen look, so white painted walls are perfect, with perhaps a natural grass paper for texture and interest on one wall.

floor

Dark-stained floorboards are ideal, but tiles also work. Mats are the traditional floor covering, but seagrass, jute, or sisal carpets are all suitable alternatives.

lighting

White or off-white lamp shades in paper, opaque parchment, or ceramic suit the theme.

storage

Closets with frosted glass or paper-faced sliding doors imitate rice-paper screens; or you might install shelves and hanging rails covered with plain white shades.

furniture

Japanese furniture is low to the ground. All you need in the bedroom is a single wooden bench and a couple of X-frame bedside stools.

accessories

Meditation on nature is at the heart of Zen—a branch of cherry blossom in a slim vase, a mound of polished pebbles in a simple dish, a beautiful Japanese landscape painting, or a calligraphy scroll on the wall.

26 girly heaven

Bright and casual, this feminine bedroom is full of pattern, texture, and fun! Colors and styles are mixed together to create a sumptuous and sexy boudoir. Whimsy and intuition are all you need to get it right.

colors

Weave a thread of continuity through the mix of colors by using a little more of one color in your palette of choice, such as lilacs and pinks or citrus and orange.

bed

Naturally, the bed is the focus, piled high with layers of pretty floral covers, quilts, and lacy pillows. Add a soft throw and a tasseled satin bolster or two. For added princess effect, surround the bed with colored and crystal-trimmed sheer draperies or panels hung from dainty poles attached to the ceiling with hooks and ribbons.

window

Cover the window with a sheer, bright panel to tint the filtered daylight. Add an outer, over-long drapery in a sumptuous fabric, and create a simple window seat padded with cushions.

walls

Paint provides the flexibility you need when you want to change one color to match another within the palette. It's a good idea not to paint all the walls in one strong color, as this will make a room feel smaller.

lighting

The lighting should be feminine and eccentric: a pretty chandelier, wall brackets with crystal droplets, strings of tiny lights circumnavigating the room, and scented candles in lanterns and colored glass holders.

floor

Because you will be spending lots of time in bare feet trying on clothes in the bedroom, it's vital to have a warm floor. Go overboard with a shag pile carpet and your feet will thank you. Alternatively, invest in large, strategically placed flokati rugs.

storage

Show off your best party dresses by displaying them on padded hangers on a coat stand or screen. If there is a shortage of closet space, stow some everyday clothing in large boxes covered in a pretty paper or fabric.

furniture

A dressing table with plenty of drawer space for cosmetics is important, of course, plus a pretty mirror, light, and an upholstered stool to sit on. Add to these a capacious bedside cabinet, a full-length swivel mirror, and a deeply comfortable "gossiping" chair.

accessories

Mount photographs together within large frames, and create a gallery space on one wall; group items of memorabilia together for display impact; store and show off pretty shoes on low open shelves.

urban loft

Imaginative zoning creates multi-functional open-plan sleeping with an integrated bath or shower room. Surprisingly, the style can be adapted to modest spaces.

space

In a large space, use low-level dividers—half-walls, large pieces of multifunctional furniture—to maintain a visual flow, or go for a change in floor level. In a more limited space, choose sliding screens or fabric hangings.

materials

Accentuate the "loft" theme with judicious use of wood, brick, and glass—brick-face on one wall with the others simply plastered and painted, glass blocks to screen a bathing area.

lighting

Keep windows clutter-free, and use overhead "bare wire" tracks that allow lights to be moved to different areas. Wall uplights will illuminate the textural qualities of the architecture.

floor

A loft is the place to be adventurous with flooring. Choose from wood, concrete, ceramic, linoleum, vinyl, and rubber, each with its pluses and minuses. Wood, for example needs regular polishing and waxing. Concrete has the right look but is noisy and heavy, so is suitable for ground-floor and basement areas only. Ceramic comes in a huge range of prices and styles, but is also noisy and heavy. Rubber is great for the loft look and maintenance is easy, but light colors show the dirt.

city slicker

"Handsome," "sophisticated," and "immaculately dressed" are the words that describe this look. Pared-down and deeply comfortable, this bedroom is functional and tailored, without frivolous decoration. It features strong materials such as wood, leather, and metal, combined with plain but tactile fabrics.

color

Dark, warm colors give an aura of comfortable sophistication. However, dark colors need to be offset with areas of light. Here, white bedding is the natural contrast. In addition, deeper colors are also lifted with touches of metallic glitz. Color combinations to set the mood:

• Charcoal, silver, and moss green
• Mushroom, midnight blue, and cream
• Plum, old gold, black, and ivory

materials

With the emphasis on masculinity, fabrics such as wide-wale corduroy, heavy linen, and wool would make a good team for the bedding. Battening some fabric to the walls will create a den-like coziness. Consider strong, tactile materials such as imitation suede or felt, defining the tailoring with a narrow ribbon along the ceiling and baseboard.

window

The tailored look could be continued with clean-cut draperies in felt or corduroy hanging from chunky poles threaded through huge eyelet holes. Alternatively, venetian blinds or louvered shutters would be equally suitable.

floor

If there is a wooden floor, you might add a touch of the West with a couple of cow-skin rugs. Leather is a luxury flooring option, and could be used as a fixed "raft" just around the bed. For a softer effect, opt for a conventional carpet that imitates sisal.

lighting

For this bachelor environment, wall-mounted lights on swivel arms might be more practical and appropriate than regular bedside lamps. Likewise, downlights and interior closet lighting do away with unnecessary freestanding lights. Don't forget the dimmer switches!

storage

The joy of living the bachelor life is that your storage can be designed to suit your suits! Make sure you have shelving that is capacious rather than over-segmented, and don't forget to include a full-length mirror in your storage planning.

bathing

With many fabrics in the room, steam from an integrated bathing area might present problems. The ideal set-up is to separate bathing areas from clothes storage with an enclosed passageway containing built-in closets and shelves. In a limited space, installing a large and powerful shower unit may be a better option than a bathtub.

29
floral update

The new floral bedroom uses light flower-patterned fabrics and solid-colored fabrics with subtle contrasting checks and stripes. Anchor it all with timeless detailing—lined and trimmed draperies, tailored cushions, and upholstered furniture.

colors

Choose well-proportioned combinations of floral colors, so that one won't dominate, or go for a single-color palette based on a toile de Jouy or a monochromatic flower design combined with a colored stripe and another small geometric pattern.
Possible floral color combinations include
• Peppermint, raspberry, and cream
• Primrose, iris blue, and snowdrop white
• Shades of lilac and aqua

materials

Shiny chintz is the classic floral fabric, but there are many modern updates such as matte cotton, linen blends, and silk. The key is lightweight fabric and the use of reflective surfaces here and there to bring out the colors' vibrancy.

pattern

Single-flower motifs look their best at windows. If the pattern is strong, don't use it again, especially if the room is on the small side, but instead choose a counter-pattern on a smaller scale for the bedspread. Cushions are a useful method of re-introducing the main floral fabrics on a small scale, or choose a cushion with a photographic botanical print. Use areas of solid-colored and neutral materials to link the florals.

floor

Flooring needs to be a strong counterpoint to the pattern and fabric. It could be as dramatic as unglazed tiles in a pale limestone color, or simply blonde wood. If you have old floorboards, you might take pity on them and strip, fill, colorwash, and varnish them. Add one of the many contemporary rugs in subtle toning colors to provide a soft touch for the feet!

retro 30

One retro-style bedroom design approach mixes flavors from various periods, rather than creating a focused period theme. This highly personalized bedroom look should evolve after the decorative foundations are in place, as it needs objects and furnishings that must be sourced from many places. The look infuses references from the twenties to the seventies, depending on preference and budget, to produce an eclectic balance. The second approach is to concentrate on a more specific period, such as the fifties, and create a bedroom theme that supports this style using the color, pattern, and texture that are appropriate to the period.

color

The best way to introduce color to a retro bedroom is through the use of decorative objects and furnishings. Anything goes, because variety is part of the look, so choose colors according to your favorite era, from pink to scarlet, acid green to luminous turquoise, or orange and brown—heaven help you! However, the more color you introduce, the less you'll need on the walls and in the flooring. To prevent the bedroom from becoming claustrophobic, keep walls and flooring mainly neutral and low-key.

walls

If you are focusing on objects from different periods, a warm, neutral color for the walls makes a safe background. Alternatively, use a subtle geometric wallpaper—softly abstract circles or rounded rectangles. Burlap wallpaper adds texture and warmth and is reminiscent of seventies style.

floor

Flooring materials are really a matter of budget and style. Black- or white-painted and varnished floorboards or plain white tiles, vinyl, parquet, square felt carpet tiles, or shag pile carpet all provide their own period reference. Otherwise, invest in a large rug whose color and design conveys the period you have chosen.

furniture and accessories

Eclectic inspiration from the twenties to the seventies might include mirrored bedside tables, a metalwork dressing table, an Arne Jacobsen-style molded plywood-and-steel chair, a multi-branched floor lamp, a melamine chest of drawers with round, tapered legs, a teak and twine ceiling light, a sunburst mirror and Savoy or "handkerchief" vases. For the bed itself, depending on period, choose a mirror-paneled headboard or a rectangular or elliptic deep-padded headboard.

31

two into one
dual-purpose bedrooms

Sometimes you have no choice but to incorporate different functions into a bedroom. The most extreme example is a studio apartment. Then there's the bedroom with shower, the bedroom that doubles as a study, and finally, the bedroom/guest room. Whichever you require, don't despair: where there is a will, there is a way of making it fit!

zone or harmonize?

If you have a lot of space, you can zone the room with half-height or full-height partitions. To minimize light loss, go for toughened, translucent glass panels, glass blocks, or a fabulous screen. Other ideas include using a freestanding shelving unit or enclosing the bed with a half-height wall that doubles as a headboard.

Alternatively, use different flooring for different activities—rubber flooring next to kitchen cabinets, for example, and hardwood and a rug for the living/sleeping area.

If space is at a premium, harmonize the room rather than zoning it. Use the same wood for cabinets in the kitchen area and the rest of the room, the same flooring material throughout, the same color theme for kitchen accessories, throws and cushions. If you keep things simple, you won't notice just how much is crammed into one small space.

conceal

In a multifunction room, some concealment is essential, which is where customized carpentry comes into its own. A small cooking or study area can be closed off behind floor-to-ceiling sliding or folding doors. Or stow your computer and keyboard on a pull-out shelf inside a cabinet or closet. If no suitable space exists, have a cabinet built in, or adapt a freestanding wardrobe to this purpose. Remember to provide for electrical and telephone connections at the outset of any construction. Add some clip-on task lighting, and you're ready for action.

use the height

Don't forget the areas above eye level. If your room has plenty of height, put your bed on a platform with storage—and perhaps a sofa—beneath. And if you've got space, you could build a room within a room. The bed is on top with steps—providing extra storage—leading from the kitchen area or bathroom (or both) downstairs. The surrounding space is dedicated to dining and relaxing.

fold, stack, and stow

Because so many new homes consist of small rooms, furniture designers have come up with some great space-saving ideas. To start with, there are good-looking fold-away and nesting tables—like your grandmother's. Then there are beds with storage beneath (see 78 and 89), as well as a whole host of stacking and folding chairs—remember the school auditorium?

32

the studio

This is the room that has it all. It's where you sleep, cook, relax, eat, and do your homework. There's no escaping it: you have to be tidy.

the bed

You may have screened off your bed or put it up on a platform (see 31), but if these options don't suit you, there are others that may. First there's the futon bed that doubles as a sofa, or the more traditional sofa bed with a foam or innerspring mattress on a wood and metal frame that simply slides and swivels into place (see 78). Finally, there's the pull-down bed in a closet that usually includes storage and sometimes a fold-down workspace, too.

fabrics

With lots of hard materials in the kitchen area, make the most of fabrics elsewhere. Velvet, corduroy, and imitation suede look sensational on the sofa or bed, and cashmere throws or a suede footstool-cum-coffee table make great finishing touches.

color

In a large bedroom, color can delineate an area—for example, a tranquil, neutral bed zone graduating to stronger tones in the study area. But if the room is small, keep the color theme unified throughout (see 31).

lighting

You need a mixture of background, task, and accent lighting, but avoid harsh solitary overhead lights. Use downlights for general and accent lighting, wall-washing uplights to expand the space, and task lights for reading and office work and for applying makeup.

pattern

You need to be careful how you use pattern, or every time you go into your studio, you'll wish you hadn't. Avoid wallpaper or fabric with a dominating pattern—it will have to fight with everything else—and instead go for restrained, symmetrical designs that will help create a decorative rhythm and be easy on the eye. Or simply stick to solid color and bring in little doses of pattern here and there.

33

bed and bath

If rebuilding our homes from scratch were possible, most of us would want another bathroom or two. The ideal second (or third) bathroom is an en-suite bath but if you don't have the space you may find room for a shower in the bedroom, or at least a sink.

where and how?

In a large bedroom, you can make an en-suite bath by adding a partition wall and a door; or, if you don't mind less privacy, you could simply have an archway. Alternatively, you might choose to break through into an adjoining room; but check with an architect first to make sure that it's safe to do so.

tiny spaces

A shower cubicle can be fitted into a very small bedroom. If you are adding some extra closets, you might consider plumbing in a shower behind a closet front for that now-you-see-it now-you-don't effect. But if a shower is really not feasible, at least fit a tiny handbasin, just for the convenience of shaving, face washing, and teeth brushing.

the wet room

For the ultimate in contemporary design, you have to have a wet room—a radical option and not to all tastes. It can either be screened from the bedroom or integrated into it. All you need is a fabulous modern shower with a securely sealed tiled floor with drainage channels. If the idea appeals to you, you must consult an architect, because there are lots of structural issues involving weight and waterproofing. If you can't bear to be parted from your bathtub, opt for a freestanding tub in the bedroom instead—claw-foot for a traditional look, or glass, wood, or steel if you're into minimalism.

the boring details

Boring they may be, but no one can afford to ignore issues of plumbing, heating, electricity, and ventilation. First, water must be brought to the new bath and waste carried away. Then you must make sure that your water heater can cope with any extra radiators (or install underfloor heating); and of course you need electricity for lighting, electrical outlets, and perhaps a towel-warming rail. And because water and electricity don't mix, you'll definitely need to use a professional installer. And last but not least, think about ventilation issues—especially if your bath doesn't have a window. You don't want unpleasant smells wafting into the bedroom, or the makeup mirror steaming up all the time.

storage

Private baths have their special storage problems; but as they say, necessity is the mother of invention. You need to think about where to keep spare towels, toilet paper, and toiletries, as well as cleaning materials and reading matter for those private moments. Think under-sink storage, clever shelving, above-the-door "dead" areas, as well as a range of decorative bowls, baskets, and boxes for a personal touch.

mixing work with pleasure

Your bedroom may be where you do a bit of paperwork, or it might be where you earn your living. Don't worry if you can't hide your equipment away or if you can't have a dedicated work area (see 31); there are other possibilities.

desk

Choose a beautiful table that doesn't necessarily say "desk." Think antique side tables, old kitchen tables, glass dining tables, even a small cloth-covered trestle table.

computer

Not all computers are boring beige bricks. Watch for sleek metal finishes, black, and juicy-fruit colors, and flat screens. There's something new every six months, so there's bound to be one that you will be proud to have on show. And if not, then read on.

screen it off

Put work out of sight and out of mind with a panel that fixes to the wall or a flexible wooden screen that snakes around awkward shapes and takes up less room than a rigid screen.

filling corners

Create a mini-workstation in a wasted corner. Build in a triangular shelf, with a cabinet beneath, as a desk; add more triangular shelves above for storage.

filing facts

Have plenty of attractive shelving, and use it to store paperwork in matching file boxes, or disguise the shelves with doors or roller shades.

health matters

Working can seriously damage your health, and there are special issues to consider if you work in your bedroom. Arrange your workstation to benefit from natural light, have good task lighting, and angle the computer screen away from the window. An ergonomic work stool is more comfortable than an ordinary chair and takes up less room. And last but not least, keep electronic equipment to a minimum, because electrical appliances emit radiation and electromagnetic fields. If possible, cables shouldn't live under the bed, nor should they trail across the floor, possibly causing someone to trip.

guest stars 35

When it comes to having a guest to stay, you may be lucky enough to have a dedicated guest bedroom, but sometimes housing a guest can entail some ingenious thinking.

the bed

In a dedicated guest room, a small double bed is adequate for a short-stay couple. A more flexible alternative is a pair of linked twin beds, stacking beds, or a twin bed with a pull-out extension. In a multipurpose room, a sofa bed, futon (see 78), or pull-down bed (see 78) may be better.

bathing

If there are no en-suite bathing facilities, a small basin in the room, lots of fluffy towels, a screen around the bathing area, and a terry bathrobe will be very welcome.

privacy

Make sure there is adequate screening at the windows, and don't forget to have a lock on the inside of the door, especially if there are bathing facilities in the room.

storage

Your guest will need to hang and fold a few clothes. Provide a small closet or, failing that, a hat stand, hooks, or a wooden garment rail.

comforts

Provide a good reading light and a task light next to a mirror. A bedside table with an alarm clock, magazines, flowers, and tissues is a nice touch.

what a squeeze!

You'd be surprised where a guest can be accommodated. Do you have a half-landing big enough to become a sleeping niche? If you do , install a mattress or foam cushions on a slatted wooden base. It can also be a window seat. To make the space more private, have curtains that enclose it.

Or have you got "dead" space under the stairs? If it's large enough, build a bed underneath, perhaps raised above some drawers and with a shelf above. Add a wall lamp for reading and a curtain for privacy.

36

the language of color

Our perception of and reaction to color is a subjective business. One person's "exquisitely subtle lilac" will be another's "wishy-washy lavender." But the reality is that different colors and the way they are used create certain moods, change a room's perspective, and subconsciously conjure up particular associations that have the most profound influence on interior style. In the bedroom context, color is pivotal in creating the right atmosphere, from cozy to cosmopolitan, soothing to sexy. Knowing how color works will help you find just the right color to suit your mood.

10 ideas

knowing your tints from your tones

- Complementary colors are diametrically opposite: red and green, yellow and violet, and blue and orange; obviously, there are lots of graduated colors between these.
- Intensity, or saturation, refers to color strength. A pure color (hue) has the highest intensity; adding gray or a complementary color will reduce intensity.
- Tint is produced by adding white to the pure color, reducing its strength: pink is a tint of red.
- Shade is produced by adding black to pure color, reducing its vividness: maroon is a shade of red.
- Tone refers to graduation from cool to warm and to lightness or darkness: pale pink to wine red, for example.

principle practice

Base, tone, and accent are the three principles of color use. The base is the most used color, the secondary color is a tone of the base, and the third is an unrelated color. Two possible palettes could be lavender, purple, and silver-gray, or putty, coffee, and brick red.

three-color trick

If you're anxious about choosing a range of colors, it's safe to stick to a three-color palette to start with and then add other colors over time as your confidence increases.

nice neutrals

Calming neutral colors come in a great range of grays, browns, beiges, and whites and would make a sophisticated bedroom choice. However, neutrals need material texture and accent color to animate the look.

keeping things simple

Monochromatic palettes are composed of one color in different guises—either in lighter or darker tones. These help the visual flow and will create a harmonious, soothing bedroom. A palette of different colors with equal tones will be harmonious and easy to use, as long as you get the subtle balance of colors right.

soothing tones

Cool colors such as violet-blues, green-blues, and blue-greens optically "recede," promoting a sense of space and serenity. Surprisingly, there are also cool pinks and yellows, but you need to have good natural and artificial light to prevent these from becoming cold.

pretty in pastel

Pastels provide a calming palette for the bedroom, but used together over a large area they can look insipid. To avoid this, anchor the palette with stronger color accents such as darker baseboards and window frames. As the palette develops, you can introduce other color accents within the soft furnishings and decoration.

deeply handsome

Dark colors such as charcoal, moss green, midnight blue, eggplant, cinnamon, and chocolate all help to create an intimate and sensuous environment. If your bedroom is naturally dark and you're not looking for the illusion of space, those colors are good bedroom choices, but set them off with some light, bright, or white contrasts.

primary colors

Intense colors such as primary yellow and red are tricky to use in the bedroom, as they optically "advance" and tend to make a small room claustrophobic. To avoid this, you could use one color on a single wall. This would usually be behind the bed to lend focus there, but there is no reason why a different wall couldn't be painted, especially if you wanted to make a strong backdrop for paintings or ornaments.

what you see is not necessarily what you get!

Always experiment with a lighter tone or two than your first choice color, because paint color will usually look darker over a large area of wall. All color is visually changed by natural light, electric lighting, texture, and surface finish, so it's a good idea to try out colors in the room before committing yourself.

neutral tones

37

Although the true neutral colors are black, white, and gray, the range used in decorating is more extensive. Best for the bedroom are warm-tinted neutrals, which include chalk, cream, bone, pearl, ivory, limestone, biscuit, parchment, sand, toffee, camel, and mushroom.

A neutral-colored bedroom is easy on the eye and promotes tranquility and relaxation. Try using different, but tonally balanced, neutrals together in varying proportions, or subtle gray and white combinations.

Introducing a minor color accent or two prevents blandness. Cushions and a bed throw are obviously versatile choices. Experimenting with any single favorite color will reveal the different effects. Charcoal or black could be the defining contrast for gray and white color schemes, perhaps for a headboard border, lampshades, or lacquered bedside tables. Pure white cotton or linen is a perfect finish for bedding. Provide visual focus with a stunning painting, flowers, or an ornate mirror.

Texture and neutrals complement each other beautifully, and attention paid to underscoring these contrasts will benefit the overall look. Try placing rough and smooth, shiny and matte, heavy and fine in juxtaposition. In addition or as an alternative to the textural focus, appropriate patterns might include muted flowing designs, such as a monochromatic crewelwork, damask, scrolling, and self-patterned fabrics and wallpapers.

With so many neutral-colored possibilities it's easy to harmonize a neutral bedroom color scheme with a private bath. Bathroom neutrals include limestone, terrazzo, marble, biscuit-glazed tiles and painted or limed tongue-and-groove paneling. Using a neutral color focus throughout helps to soften and blend hard edges and surfaces.

The bedroom is a perfect environment for mixing neutral colors, pattern, and texture because there are so many elements to associate them with without upseting the decorative rhythm. Mix them with earthy materials such as stone, wicker, bamboo, and rattan; fabrics like linen, silk, and mohair; and organic flooring such as sisal and seagrass.

38

fresh shades

The fresh bedroom look is based on crisp, clean, light colors that are carefree, restorative, and easy on the eye.

Combined with lots of white, shades of blue and green work well together when they are of the same tonal range. Try painting the walls in blocks of chalky blue, aqua, and lilac for a soft patchwork effect, or use the colors on walls, ceiling, painted furniture, and architectural detailing.

Blue and white are always a popular combination, as are the sunshine colors yellow and blue; but choose these with care—a primrose yellow with a red-touched blue—or the yellow can look quite cold. You might introduce some elements of gray as a tempering influence.

Metallic and shiny finishes are good companions for the fresh color palette. Silver paint can be "tinted" with an undercoat of lilac or blue, revealed when the silver is "rubbed off" slightly.

Fabrics must be light to maintain the freshness of the look. Go for solid-colored lightweight taffeta, silk blends, and sheers for windows and dressing the bed. Pattern must be unfussy—a crisp, simple flower print, a two-toned geometric, an unfussy floral motif, along with solids, checks, and stripes for upholstery and cushions.

Artificial lighting needs the brightness of halogen downlights combined with soft wall-washing from low-level uplights.

A sense of space and light is best maintained by having simple window treatments—unlined fabric panels with tab tops in a sheer or patterned print are a good choice—and minimal ornamentation. However, mirrored furniture or oversized mirrors on the wall will reflect and accentuate the room's light and color.

bright shades

We associate bright colors with exotic travel to India, Morocco, Mexico, and the Caribbean. The color range includes the three primaries—red, blue and yellow—and a host of shades in between, from hot pink to orange, lettuce green to turquoise, banana yellow to imperial purple.

You could choose a single color such as cornflower blue or lacquer red as the principal player, perhaps painted on one wall and outlined with a darker color. Paint or paper the other walls in a neutral shade—silver gray as a counterpoint to the red, biscuit to the blue. For a softer, subtler look, create your own colors in tinted acrylic or oil glaze, which gives you control over the intensity of color and a depth to the finish that is lacking in standard water-based paint.

A brightly colored palette is fun, but you must take care in small spaces

and where the light is cold, because bright colors will decrease the sense of space. You will also need plenty of versatile electric lighting, because bright colors can look heavy in low, flat light.

Bright colors can also be used against a relatively neutral background. Introduce them in your bed linen, cushions, throws, lamps, and decorative objects.

Another way to use bright color is on window frames, baseboards, and doors; or for a fun contemporary look, choose an unusual floor covering, such as rubber tiles, in a vivid color.

Hot, bright color generates vitality and creativity, so it's good for a working area in a bedroom. If nothing else, you might choose a brightly colored desk chair and filing accessories.

And finally, as a foil, always include ample areas of neutral color. The floor is the obvious place—think wood, glazed tiles, or woven sisal for a strong but cool visual base.

dark tones

Dark, moody colors give a bedroom a sophisticated look. This color range includes charcoal, ash gray, moleskin, cinnamon, chocolate, midnight blue, moss green, plum, damson, and eggplant. Choose dark colors to cocoon a small bedroom that is lacking in natural light, or use them as a dramatic backdrop for imaginative bedding and glamorous furniture and ornaments.

Dark colors complement other dark colors to spectacular effect, but benefit from lighter, brighter touches to maximize their impact and vigor and prevent any hint of oppressiveness. Introduce white or neutral elements and touches of "sparkle" in the form of contrasting color, metallic detailing, and creative lighting. Effective palettes to consider include
• Prussian blue walls; charcoal, midnight blue, and white bedding with metallic gray cushions;

charcoal paintwork with antique silver highlights in furniture and architectural details. Greyhound gray-and-blue bordered felt draperies hung from antiqued silver-painted poles. Pigeon-gray carpet.
• Damson glaze-finished walls or a wine-red damask wallpaper; flat black woodwork; wood louvered blinds or shutters; old gold highlights in ornamental detail; ivory bedding with chocolate covers; floorboards in similar wood finish as blinds or shutters.
• Ivy green mid-sheen painted walls or a wallpaper with a flowing two-tone green pattern; mushroom and coffee with cream bedding; mushroom velvet draperies; bronze finishing details and accessories; natural flooring such as jute or sisal.

If you use dark color in a vertical block—for instance, on a single wall—you could reintroduce it in a horizontal form, as an area rug or a bedspread, for example, and add another touch or two elsewhere, such as a couple of cushions and a lampshade. These small details are perfect for helping to settle the eye

and create visual rhythm.

The effect of lighting on dark color can be spectacular. Use floor-mounted uplights in corners to ensure that the dark color doesn't end up black. Small downlights provide sparkle, while spotlights focus on decorative objects or paintings (see 56). Bedside lighting might be wall-mounted sconce lamps or bedside table lights (see 55). And don't forget the magic of candlelight gleaming on lustrous dark walls and catching the metallic highlights.

41 muted tones

Muted colors are generally created with a touch of black or gray added to the base color. For bedroom use, the most suitable colors include dusty rose, plaster pink, sage green, French gray, and Swedish blue. These colors are naturally

affiliated with French châteaux and Swedish homesteads. There are other kindred colors, including earthy mustard, terracotta, and Shaker blue-green, but they are rather heavy for bedroom decoration.

French gray is somewhere between gray, blue, and green, which makes an easy-on-the-eye background color for walls. Dusty rose partners this color beautifully as draperies and bed covers. To emphasize the French theme, you might use a toile de Jouy, a pictorial print usually depicting 18th-century pastoral scenes. Alternatively, select embroidery weaves or small florals that have plenty of white in them.

A sleigh bed or "boat bed" would be ideal, hung with checked or flower-sprig silk draperies from a ceiling "corona" (see 82). To complete the château look, include white painted furniture with gilt detailing,

large rococo-style mirrors, candlelight sconces and a crystal chandelier. Alternatively, create a fusion look with thoroughly modern furniture in pale wood and glass. The floor could be painted white or sanded with an Aubusson-style needlepoint rug in dusty rose and sage green tones.

Alternatively, the muted scheme could be developed using Swedish blue as its foundation color. Paint the walls matte bone white, and create "frames" of gray-blue in varying widths of stripe-within-stripe as a fantasy paneling effect. The curtain or drapery fabric could be a combined stripe and flower motif to fall in loose lengths onto the floor. A bed with a decorative wooden high head- and footboard would suit the look, dressed with a puffy comforter with a blue-and-white check. Furniture could follow the theme but extend the coloring in blonde wood or white and sage green paint. Bleached wooden flooring could be softened with white cotton runners or a natural-weave rug bound around the edges with contrasting fabric.

42
talk about texture

Texture is as significant as color and pattern to good interior design. Textures can be combined in many ways, and in fact, bedrooms and en-suite baths are ideal for maximizing the use of texture, because there is so much variety of materials to play with (see 43).

looking for texture

You may be surprised to learn that texture is everywhere. It is found not only in fabrics but in paint finishes, wallpaper, carpeting, leather, metal, wood, brick, stone, and glass—so indulge!

the elements of texture

Texture can be rough, smooth, opaque, sheer, matte, or glossy and can also be divided into "cool" and "warm." Cool textures include smooth, light-reflective surfaces such as satin, silk, gloss paint, glazed tiles, and glass; warm ones include matte, light-absorbing surfaces—linen, mohair, imitation suede, limestone, and natural wood are good examples.

keep hold

Some colors—neutrals for instance—"hold" texture better than others.

textural pattern

Texture creates its own pattern and can introduce a sense of geometry and balance.

sensuosity

Exploit a material's texture—put velvet, silk, or lambswool on the bed so you can touch it; or have an open-weave linen panel at the window so light filtering through creates a pattern on the floor.

bath texture

Hard textures such as tile, metal, and porcelain inevitably dominate in a bathroom, so include some softening ones for contrast—rush matting and bath mats, towels, and sheer curtains.

restrictions apply

In the bedroom, restrict the use of hard materials such as stone, brick, and tiles to maintain a sense of peace and harmony.

light

Textures look different according to the light. Flat lighting diminishes their subtlety. Uplights and sidelighting are most effective.

textural links

For a textural link between the bedroom and en-suite bath, make use of textural echoes. Have the same wood for bedroom furniture and bathroom cabinets, or matte and glossy paint in the same color and proportions. Or differentiate the two zones with hard, glossy surfaces for the bathroom and soft and matte materials in the bedroom.

dampening off

The dampness of the bathroom puts many textural fabrics and soft flooring materials out of bounds, but enjoy those that don't mind getting damp around the edges, such as luxurious terrycloth and rush flooring.

10 ideas

texture in the bedroom and the en-suite bath

fabric choices

The bed naturally serves as the main stage on which to use textured fabrics, but lots of different ones together can just be too much. Choose one or two as highlights and use only for cushions or upholstery.

on the wall

Wall coverings offer another huge range of textural possibilities. Depending on the look you want in the bedroom, choose from grass fiber, burlap, metallic and matte-textured wallpapers, contrasting matte and sheen paint or suede-effect paint, and polished plaster. Bathroom choices include tile, stone, and metal cladding and wood. Combinations of clear and etched glass and mirror are also effective.

take the floor

In the bedroom the choices include wood, tiles, leather, and rubber, all of which can be softened with rugs or mats. Natural floorings include sisal, jute, seagrass, thick tatami, or thin Goza mats (see 69). In the bath, exploit hard flooring—terrazzo and mosaic for texture with pattern, slate with its subtle ridges. Textured rubber is practical as well as visually interesting. And don't forget the fluffy bath mat!

textural combinations for that "wow!" factor

44

Finding the right partnerships among textured ingredients should be as much fun as mixing color and pattern. The joy of using texture in the bedroom—not forgetting that textures are found in wall finishes, flooring, and hard components as well as fabrics—is in finding just the right combinations for a tactile and sensuous mix that underlines your individual bedroom style. So don't feel restrained in your choices, but seek out interesting, even eccentric, ingredients to give your look a designer's edge.

updated deco

For a contemporary echo of twenties Art Deco, which plays on matte and shiny surfaces:
• Painted matte-and-luster horizontally striped walls
• Modern abstract appliqué draperies
• Satin quilt
• Mirrored furniture
• Stripped matte-varnished floorboards
• Self-patterned mixed-pile rug

urban loft

Tactile but strong textural combinations wrapped up in a shell of gleaming plaster:
• Polished plaster walls
• wide-wale corduroy draperies
• Wool and suede on the bed

• Contrasting-colored wide-wale corduroy and tweed cushions with bone buttons
• Luxurious loop-pile carpeting

morocco bound

Keep a richly textural but neutral background and make the bed the focus of brightly colored mixed-media textures:
• Parchment-effect wallpaper
• Sheer, bright fabric hanging behind the bed
• Patterned silk bedspread
• Mirrored and fringed fabric for cushions and satin-tasseled bolsters
• Fretwork window screens
• Jute carpet on patterned tiled floor

new damask and silk

Damask's allover pattern makes a handsome textural partner for sensational "creased" fabrics at the window:
• Modern damask-style wallpaper
• "Creased" silk fabric draperies
• Imitation-suede-covered bed
• Satin sheets, wool blankets

matte and shiny

A neutral palette allows textural contrasts to play against each other for maximum effect:
• Grass-fiber wallpaper
• Wooden slatted window blinds
• Neutral-colored satin headboard
• Matelassé quilt
• Animal-skin print carpet

45

play with pattern

Pattern is complex. We react intuitively to it, so make your response your starting point. If you like a dominant pattern, use it to dictate the room's style, or choose a pattern that is easily integrated in a variety of looks.

bedroom choices

Bedroom fabrics offer plenty of pattern opportunities. Obvious favorites are florals, checks, and stripes, but pattern is also in textural fabrics such as chenille, quilting, and matelassé. Finally, there are fabrics such as lace and printed or appliqué sheers which need light to reveal their pattern.

pattern partners

Proportion and harmony are key for successful pattern marriages. Stripes, checks, and florals are natural partners, while dot, lozenge, and small motifs

socialize with almost any larger pattern. Toile de Jouy, crewelwork, and chinoiserie usually take center stage.

showing style

Pattern helps to signpost a particular decorative style. A muted floral fabric leads it in one direction, a sassy geometric wallpaper in another.

in a mood

Pattern helps create a certain mood, whether sensuous, playful, dramatic, feminine, masculine, cozy, or sophisticated. Emphasize the effect by your choice of color and texture—dark, matte, and heavy for masculine; pastel, shiny, and translucent for feminine.

color coding

Pattern is easier to use when the color range is restricted. For a restrained, harmonious look, use neutral-colored, subtle patterns such as stamped and appliquéd fabrics, damask, and monochrome crewelwork.

creating rhythm

Bedroom patterns should be easy on the eye, so go for symmetrical or

repetitive designs and broad horizontal lines rather than busy pattern.

proportional representation

Depending on their size, stripes can elongate or diminish length and width, while a bold design will break up a large expanse of wall.

pattern as a disguise

Rhythmically patterned wallpaper such as toile de Jouy or a flowing floral design will disguise a room's awkward angles.

finding focus

Pattern can lead the eye around the room and draw it to a focal point. It can also appear discreetly in lampshades, cushions, upholstery, or a decorative vase or rug.

tile claustrophobia

Avoid an excess of patterned tiles in an en-suite bath, or the effect will be claustrophobic. Bear in mind that the smaller the tiles, the more "pattern" there will be.

10 rules

46 put pattern in its place

how much can you take?

If you have a large bedroom, combine a dominant wallpaper pattern with smaller patterns for cushions, pillowcases, or upholstery. At the other extreme, a small wallpaper pattern won't make a small room bigger but can make you feel dizzy, so use it on just one wall and paint the others in a harmonizing color.

creating an aura

Correlate your favorite pattern with your chosen style: striped florals with gray-green paintwork and gilt detailing for a French boudoir look; paisley and crewelwork with colored muslin, beading, and metallic thread to evoke an Indian theme. For a modern retro style, use a limited amount of dots, circles, or spots, either as a wall or a fabric pattern, and fill in with color and texture choices that underline the theme.

pattern v. plain

When bold, colorful patterns are used together, include some soothing accents of white, gray, beige or black. In conjunction with single-colored walls use boldly patterned fabrics generously, but if the walls are patterned, stick to solid-colored fabrics. Even a single element of bold pattern—used on a stool cover or bed throw for example—will give a decorative edge to an otherwise plain look.

shape and line

Diagonal patterns such as trellis- or latticework give the illusion of width and height, while vertical and horizontal stripes emphasize height and length respectively (see 49). Pattern can be used discreetly for definition—for example, a Greek key pattern or a simple plaid (see 49) used as a border can liven up a plain wood floor or carpet.

alternative pattern

Pattern is found not just in fabrics and wallpapers but also in stone and wood flooring, in the pattern of a woven chair back or the geometric layout of bricks and tiles. And don't forget the pattern of sunlight through slatted blinds or the shadow shapes on walls created by atmospheric lighting. Ornaments and pictures contribute pattern, too.

pattern tips

Before choosing any pattern, consider the pattern repeat and how a design will look when hung. Floral designs are particularly likely to turn out looking like columns (see 50). It's useful to know that a bold design on a lightweight fabric, such as silk or sheer, provides a quite different look from the same pattern on velvet or coarse linen.

bath patterns

Geometric designs, such as single motif and Islamic shapes, with their soothingly repetitive rhythm, work well on bathroom tiles. However, the repetitive pattern of tiles is difficult to visualize, so lay out a few sets of tiles to see how they look in a block before buying them. You can also create focused areas of pattern by using mosaic tiles as backsplashes for the sink and bathtub.

47 fabric fantasy

Fabric is fundamental to the comfort of your bedroom, but it also conveys style and ambiance. We all have our personal likes and dislikes, but here are some suggestions for top fabrics that might find favor in your room.

windows

For winter warmth, try velvet, corduroy, or wool felt (see 59), but if your style is light and airy or you want to vary the effect in summer, turn to a silk blend or unlined linen.

sheers

The drab nylon glass curtains of yesteryear have thankfully given way to a multitude of delightful sheer fabrics. Plain cotton voile is perfectly acceptable, but why not think about the new metallic-shot sheers or sheers with an embossed or woven pattern?

on the walls

Fabric on the walls insulates well and creates a cocooned and cozy bedroom (see 77, 81, 82). Among the best fabrics to use are felt or baize, crewelwork, or toile de Jouy.

sheets

Egyptian cotton is popular, and Irish linen has a unique look and tactile attraction, but for pure sensuosity, nothing beats silk satin (see 83).

pillowcases

Pillowcases to match your sheets are usually a first choice, but if you have extra pillows for a luxurious-looking bed, you might contrast-cover them in a fabric used elsewhere in the room (see 83).

bedcovers

Pure Merino wool or mohair blankets are expensive but hard to beat for quality; a less expensive choice is a soft fleece fabric. If you have sheets and blankets, you might need a matelassé cotton figured quilt and could finish the look off with a faux fur or soft fleece (see 83).

headboards

Contemporary headboards are more about visual effect than head support (see 81). For tactility there's imitation suede; for fashionability, denim, corduroy, tweed, or satin; but for practicality make washable linen-cotton blend slipcovers.

cushions

Cushions provide an excuse to indulge in a small amount of opulence. Consider mixing faux fur, cashmere, and silk, or embroidery, appliqué, and dévoré (see 83).

upholstery

An elegant easy chair, stool, or sofa—if you've got room—might be covered in damask or stamped velvet, but for something more edgy, why not try faux animal skin?

bathroom choice

It's difficult to include luxurious fabrics in a bathroom, in case they rot or stain. Instead, stick to practical, washable fabrics such as cotton and terrycloth. For a touch of luxurious texture you could include some ribbed or combed-cotton bath sheets.

10 ideas

48 special-effect fabrics

Among the myriad fabrics, including the purely decorative and the essentially practical, some stand out as making a special contribution to the bedroom scene. These might be considered for their specific sensuous, tactile character, because they are a little out of the ordinary, or because, even in small quantities, they add to the room's decorative attributes.

• Pinstripe and wool bedcovers and upholstery for a tailored, masculine look

• Felt for no-sew curtains hung from poles through oversized grommets

• Dévoré or stamped velvet for sensuous texture as a bedspread or throw

• Faux fur lined in velvet or suede-effect fabric for a decadently deluxe bedspread

• Permanent-pleat draperies of silk or silk-effect blend for the way it shimmers and hangs without the need for heading tape

• Voile with metallic threadwork lines or patterns to shimmer at the window or use as an alternative headboard hanging

• Satin for adding a contrasting border to anything textural, from a bedspread to cushions and draperies

• Cashmere for the softest and most luxurious extra bed pillows

• Burlap for inexpensive earthy companions to stone, tiles, and wood

• Tweed for its novelty, subtle color range, and adaptability to the non-sexist bedroom

checks, plaids, stripes

Among the most easily put together and versatile of combinations, checks, plaids, and stripes are great for bedrooms.

exclusive use

If you use stripes, plaids, and checks on their own, "anchor" them with areas of solid color or neutral space somewhere in the bedroom.

livening up

For a cosmopolitan look, use a stripe, check, or plaid in a taffeta, silk, or moiré. These patterns are also sophisticated with a decorative trim such as ribbon, fringe, or braid. Pinstripes and checked shirt cottons combine well with other fabrics to create a tailored, masculine bedroom.

simple or complex

Checked and plaid patterns can be as simple as gingham or as complex and multicolored as tartan. A complex plaid used on one wall only will be easy on the eye, especially if any pictures are lined up with the checks.

big and little

Curtains or shades in a large plaid could be lined and bordered with a smaller version. Stripes, checks, and plaids can be used to line bed hangings or simply used unlined as the hangings themselves.

lining it up

Striped wallpaper makes a good partner to floorboards, as the lines echo each other. Striped fabric can also be cut to emphasize the contours of upholstered furniture and tailored bedding. Be very sparing with bright and trendy "bar-code" stripes for bedroom use—they're fun, but very busy.

composite stripes

Stripes are also part of more complex designs such as brocade and serpentine floral patterns, which add extra pattern dimension and color. These are most suitable for a classic French- or Italian-oriented scheme.

scale and stripes

The scale of wall stripes should be judged by their color contrast and the spatial dimensions involved. The closer and narrower the stripes, the louder the contrast and the more the area they cover will visually close in.

checking out the bathroom

A bathroom is ideal for using checks and diamonds, thanks to the geometric shape of wall and floor tiles. For example, you could create a large checkerboard or diamond pattern in tiles to define the shower or bathtub area.

50 the greatest fabric combos ever

There are certain bedroom partnerships that are destined to go exceedingly well together, if only they can be introduced under the right circumstances and are given a favorable environment. A well-chosen fabric will underscore the bedroom theme, and when one appropriate fabric is used in juxtaposition with another, the partnership, as in cooking, can be sublime. You don't need to employ an interior designer to conjure up delicious fabric mixes; just take your inspiration from the pages of magazines and the offerings below.

on safari

If you like the natural and tactile attributes of an African interior, adapt them to an urban environment:
• Bed runner and cushions made from African Kente cloth (basket-weave strip cloth with symbolic patterns)
• Indigo blue raw silk square-quilted and tuft-buttoned bedspread
• Natural muslin curtains with a blue-and-black cotton border

bright and beautiful

Remember that it's not only the fabric alone, but also what you do with it that counts. It's easy to make wool felt interesting with pinking shears, and here it accompanies contrasting fabrics of satin and herringbone for a light-hearted but still bedroomy look:
• Lime-green felt draperies with pinked zigzag edges
• Black/gray/green-patterned linen-cotton blend bedspread
• Gray and black felt and satin cushions with pinked edges
• Herringbone black/white upholstery

french dressing

For some reason shiny yellow, chocolate, and matte gray work fabulously well together. This scheme has a French influence:
• Yellow damask draperies with broad chocolate trim
• Gray velvet bedspread with chocolate satin scalloped border
• Embroidery and linen cushions
• Square-and-flower motif upholstery

pictures and posies

Toile de Jouy, gingham, roses, and lace are classic partners:
• Red toile de Jouy bedspread trimmed with gingham
• Cotton- and lace-trimmed sheets and pillowcases
• Rosebud chintz draperies with contrasting green border
• Large plaid for upholstery

highland fling

It can be difficult to find fabric combinations that appeal to both partners in the bedroom, but this is one that should:
• Paisley-print bedspread
• Fern green chenille throw
• Tartan taffeta cushions
• Curtains in a striped silk in heather, gray, and fern green
• Heather-colored tweed upholstery, trimmed with leather

51

second-hand rose

The floral motif has long been a popular bedroom choice, but today's designs cover a far more versatile spectrum of reference and style, much influenced by innovative fabric technology and production techniques.

• Two or three different floral patterns can be used together, but care is needed not to suffocate the room. Plenty of solid color will prevent this.

• Some floral and leaf designs suit a masculine bedroom, to contrast with purposefully male ingredients such as leather and black lacquer. Examples are abstract monochromatic designs, rich damasks, and jacquard woven patterns.

• Use a large, graphic floral pattern as a single wallpapered wall; add a small scale flower design plus a stripe, check, or plaid. Use these to contrast line or border each other.

• Explore the modern potential of crisp and unfussy floral pattern with sleek furniture, contemporary flooring materials, and lots of space.

• Hang light, floral curtains when spring arrives and change them for something darker, heavier, and cozier for the winter months.

• Use an allover floral design for walls, ceiling, and curtains or shades in a small room to create a charmingly cocooned haven.

• Modern chintzes are often produced with an artificially aged finish, which softens the colors and produces a more informal, harmonious effect.

• Note how color influences the effect of a pattern. A faded pale-pink flower conveys a different mood from a bold purple one.

• You can use the same small floral pattern in different colorways together, as long as they are within the same balanced tonal range.

• A large-scale lifelike botanical print is best shown off as a flat window or wall panel. If the window is wider than the fabric, add a contrasting fabric border.

keep it practical 52

Certain fabrics are special to the bedroom because their unique, practical qualities and specific in-bedroom contribution elevate them above others, which rely on fashion, whim, or budget.

cotton

Cotton comes in different weights, textures, and colors. It's tough and resilient and combines well with other fabrics. It is also anti-static and cool to sleep in; Egyptian cotton is a top-quality choice for bed sheets. Although it might need more vigorous ironing than cotton-blend fabric, it washes, wears, and feels better. Cotton terrycloth, with its pile of uncut loops, is the ideal fabric for towels; a generous piece of this, bound at the edges, makes a luxurious bath sheet.

linen

Linen has a unique touch and texture and is sometimes mixed with cotton to increase its suppleness. It ages well and comes in a great range of subtle colors and designs. It combines easily with other fabrics and can be used for window treatments, bed dressing, upholstery, or slipcovers.

silk

Silk is the finest, smoothest, and strongest natural fiber. It takes dye well and comes in a wide range of exceptionally beautiful colors. It isn't susceptible to mildew, nor will dry cleaning damage it. However, in time, strong sunlight will make it fade and deteriorate, so it is best located away from bright light. Even in a small quantity, such as for cushions or a wall panel, it adds eye-catching quality.

polarfleece

Although this is a synthetic fabric, its qualities of warmth and softness make it practical and comforting as blankets, throws, and cushions. Also, it comes in a good range of bright and subtle colors—and is inexpensive, too.

felt

Felt doesn't fray, and so it can be left unhemmed and simply cut and shaped as required. Its structural quality makes it an unusual drapery fabric and looks both smart and tactile when used for upholstery and cushions.

53

make light work of lighting

A well-planned lighting system will highlight the bedroom's decorative assets, will be practical, and will help create the desired mood. The three types of lighting you will need are background, task, and accent lighting. Especially in a bedroom, the secret of success is flexibility, so that you can switch instantly from bright and functional to moodily atmospheric. Using today's sophisticated systems and cutting-edge design, bedroom illumination can be subtle and atmospheric or sensationally decorative, according to your needs.

getting enough

It's wise to install more lighting than you think you'll need, wiring the various types to different dimmer switches. Darker-colored rooms need extra lighting because dark color absorbs light, particularly if the walls are a matte finish.

lighting to wash by

This is a plea for atmospheric lighting in the bathroom. Naturally, there must be practical lighting, too, but the bathroom should be a relaxing, self-indulgent retreat with two independent types of lighting: one practical, the other atmospheric.

the right bulb

Incandescent bulbs, the regular creamy yellow filament lightbulbs, are sometimes tinted for mood effect. Halogen lights provide a whiter, crisper light. Their sparkle makes them good as uplights, downlights, spots, and accent lights. Fluorescent tubes emit a hard light unless they are installed behind a special opaque baffle, which will act to soften the glare.

natural light

Strong natural light is more invigorating and beneficial than artificial light. Sunlight can be exploited by clearing the window area as much as possible and positioning furniture so that the natural light can be enjoyed while getting up or relaxing in the afternoon. If your natural light is poor, create a warm, inward-looking atmosphere with dark colors and lots of adaptable electric lighting.

lightly balanced

It's important to minimize areas of harsh shadow in the bedroom, since they disturb the visual flow and create a sense of unease. Lighting

distributed evenly around the room at different levels will help prevent this.

getting in the mood

The more flexible and user-friendly the lighting control system, the easier it will be to create atmosphere on demand. Switches with dimmers should be placed by the door and at either side of the bed. Don't forget candlelight—for its scent as well as romance.

seeing the light

Requirements for bedroom task lighting are for reading, working, applying and removing makeup, and seeing into closets and drawers.

in the background

In a bedroom, background or ambient lighting is the least used, its main function being to smooth out harsh angles and shadows. If you choose a central ceiling light, do so for the decorative, rather than practical, contribution it will make to the room.

different accents

Fixed accent lighting reduces the flexibility you have for changing the bedroom's layout or the way you have arranged pictures and ornaments. You should, of course, provide accent lighting for display shelves that are permanent, but freestanding lights or clip-ons will be more versatile.

checking positions

The positioning of lights can be manipulated to eliminate hard shadows and glare. Before you make any final decisions, how about checking what the lights will look like from the lying-on-the-bed perspective?

54

lighten up

For comfortable, unobtrusive illumination that eliminates shadows in the bedroom, background lighting needs to spread the light broadly downward and upward. Use separate dimmer switches to give control over the individual elements.

ceiling lights

A single pendant light can create a bland or glaringly unflattering light and should be considered only when its decorative benefit exceeds its lighting contribution.

five ceiling lights to suit

1 • The classic paper lantern, appropriate for a minimalist or Zen bedroom
2 • A chandelier
3 • The star lantern for an ethnic-styled bedroom
4 • Abstract sculptural shapes associated with contemporary interiors
5 • A multi-branched "Octopus" light to suit a retro bedroom look.

sconces

Candlelight sconces are a source of soft ambient light and elegance, especially in pairs flanking a handsome mirror.

wall washers and floor lights

Low-level uplights create a soothing environment, will enhance the texture of the wall, and will highlight architectural detail.

downlights

Small downlights in the ceiling provide even background light. They look dramatic fitted around the perimeter of the room only and linked to dimmer switches.

lamps

Well-placed table and floor lamps at different heights and linked to dimmer switches create the most balanced and harmonious background lighting. The light can be manipulated by choosing lampshades with reflective colored linings; gold, for instance, will ensure a warm radiance. Shades and bases need to be carefully matched for style and size.

55

practical lighting

Practical bedroom lighting can be achieved either by installing discreet fixtures when you build the room or by having add-on light fixtures that reflect the bedroom style.

reading lights

A bedside light should be high enough to throw light onto a book without causing any glare. Space-saving designs include wall-mounted reading lights on swivel arms; or, if you are commissioning an oversized headboard, have the lighting incorporated in it. A pivoting floor lamp is versatile, as it could be moved to provide task lighting in another area of the room.

vanity lighting

Lights on either side of the dressing table or wall-mounted mirror provide even, glare-free illumination, but you could also place your dressing table so natural light will fall on your face. You'll need adequate light for all that time in front of the long mirror, too!

closet lighting

Lighting that comes on automatically when you open a closet is very convenient, while lighting behind opaque door panels reduces the visual bulk of a large area of wardrobes.

work lighting

A single halogen desk lamp with a pivoting arm is adequate for a small work area. If you have shelves above your work area, you could install small downlights behind a lip in the bottom shelf.

lighting an en-suite bath

Mirror lights are most efficient on either side of the mirror. Halogen downlights provide sparkling crisp light; position them so you can read in the bath. As an extra, atmospheric light can be provided by lights set behind glass blocks in the wall or behind custom-designed baffles, and if you have the room, don't forget groups of small candles on the ledge around the bathtub.

56
display lighting

Accent or display lighting creates directional highlights that illuminate objects, pictures, an interesting architectural detail, or a piece of furniture. They add another layer to the bedroom lighting environment.

uplights

Miniature uplights hidden in lipped shelving units will discreetly illuminate decorative items. Larger uplights can be placed at floor level in front or behind objects to dramatic effect. This method of lighting also has the advantage of eliminating any dark corners in the room.

downlights

Swivel downlights with a narrow beam partially recessed into the ceiling direct light onto a particular area or object. Alternatively, they can be attached to the underside of a shelf and concealed by a lip.

spotlights

To illuminate a single item, a clip-on or lamp-stand spotlight will give mobility and variable control. Most modern spotlights take incandescent reflector bulbs with silver interiors or low-voltage halogen bulbs with integrated reflectors to project light and disperse heat backward.

track lighting

For a studio apartment, track lighting, with individual lamps that can focus on specific areas, provides a degree of versatility. It can be "floated" in a high-ceilinged area without interfering with the visual flow, because it runs on unobtrusive thin wires.

picture lights

If you have a special work of art to draw attention to, you can illuminate it with an integrated picture light; but note that this works best without glass, as there can be glare from the reflection. However, an integrated picture light commits you to a certain lighting position. An alternative is a miniature ceiling-mounted picture light with a focused beam that fits the object precisely; however, these are expensive.

invasion of privacy what to do with your windows

Privacy needs in the bedroom go further than merely shielding our private lives from the neighbor opposite! We also need to consider privacy in relation to sex, bathing, dressing, and undressing—and if streetlights or daylight disturb your sleep, you may want to block out all the light.

taking shape

Sometimes the look of a bedroom is driven by a window's style. For example, a dormer window doesn't lend itself to a Zen-style look, and panoramic floor-to-ceiling windows don't conjure up a Nordic-inspired bedroom. In such cases, you may have to go for a look that incorporates the window's idiosyncrasies.

With a neutral window, you can match the window treatment to your decorative theme. A valance and draperies that puddle onto the floor suit a boudoir-style room, while an oriental-themed bedroom might have fine linen shades. Floral draperies, hung from a pole with bow ties over lace curtains, partner an utterly feminine bedroom.

5 ideas

sheer folly

Sheer curtains alone allow you to look out on the world during the day without being seen, but the effect will be reversed at night (see 48). A roller shade behind the curtains will serve for nighttime privacy in this situation.

lining benefits

Naturally, the thicker the curtain or drapery material, the more light it will exclude, but to optimize light and sound exclusion draperies can be interlined or lined with light-blocking material. There are also shades with a special backing treatment that cuts out light. An alternative is a Roman shade made from a light-restricting material such as a dark, heavy woven fabric or imitation suede. An aluminum or wood venetian blind will also screen out light fairly effectively.

on valance

Valances can be girly and beguiling in feminine, floral bedrooms and work particularly well with lightweight fabrics and sheers. They can also be paired with a shaped cornice board to add a soft outline to the window.

changing perspectives

To add height to the bedroom, fix a fabric valance or covered cornice board well above the top of the window frame, so that the curtain/drapery drop is extended; to visually broaden a window, hang your draperies well outside the window frame. In a bedroom where you wish to maximize the sense of space, allow draperies to fall in straight folds to the floor. This will extend the vertical dimension and help maintain visual continuity.

58

window dressing

It's very easy to get carried away with the aesthetic enjoyment of beautiful decorator fabrics and trimmings or innovative alternative window treatments, but the priorities for bedroom window dressing should be more practical.

• When making your own window treatments from washable fabric, allow extra length for shrinkage, or pre-wash the fabric.

• If you've fallen for an expensive fabric and can't afford to use it for conventional draperies, buy just enough for a single panel to hang straight to the floor, adding borders to make up the window width if necessary. This especially suits large-scale floral or photoprint designs, as you can see the whole motif.

• For an unobstructed view from the window, combined with privacy, take "half-measures." Try hanging "café" curtains across the lower half of the window or installing half shutters.

• Lining draperies with a tiny motif-printed cotton, gingham, or ticking fabric provides an attractive view of the draperies that can be enjoyed by people looking in from the outside.

• If your drapery headings are going to be on view, contrast-bind them for a defined finish.

• Personalize ready-made draperies by adding borders, trims, appliqué, ribbon, or buttons; or enliven a plain purchased shade with appliqué, stencils, or a stick-on ribbon border.

• For unusual tiebacks, think wire, jute, leather, or even a pair of decorative belts.

59

heavy draperies run for cover

Heavy draperies are cozy—good for cold winter nights and bad views. They also insulate against light, sound, and pollution. Velvet, wool blends, linen, and corduroy are substantial fabrics, while silk, taffeta, and chintz are ideal for a lighter, romantic style. Whatever fabric you choose, heavy draperies will eat up a large chunk of your budget, and you won't really want to change them again for a while, so think long-term adaptable rather than this year's fad.

something different

• Unlined wool felt hangs in accordion folds from giant metal eyelets
• Plaid woolen blankets with frayed edges finished with grosgrain ribbon
• Antique quilts; if one isn't big enough, use two, cut and sewn in alternate strips
• Waffle cotton bedspreads with tab tops
• Dress or suit fabrics (narrower than decorator fabric). Try herringbone or hounds-tooth check, lined with cotton fabric, for a masculine look. For a more feminine version, use a nubby bouclé in lavender or heather pink edged with moiré silk.

60 sheer excitement

With a range of revolutionary fabrics, superb colors, and adventurous weaves, unlined lightweight window curtains and draperies are very much back in fashion.

The beauty of sheers is in the fabric, rather than the heading. Although they can be used for draperies, with pleated headings, they are more often made into curtains, with a cased heading that slips over a rod, gathering up the fabric. A small fold of fabric above the casing forms a ruffle. A pin-tucked heading is a more elaborate alternative. Or you could simply tie the fabric to a pole or wooden dowel with satin ribbons.

Sheers don't need fancy or heavy-duty hardware, either. You have the choice of ties, tabs, hooks, rings, clips, or eyelets used with plastic-coated wire or tension wire, or with metal, Lucite, or wooden rods.

sheer style

• Some weaves are loose or delicately worked and make a change from pure white sheers. For contrast, you could add a border of slinky satin silk or velvet.
• "Parachute" silk and linen make fine partners when they're sewn together in horizontal bands with bands of drawn thread work between them to allow maximum fluidity. Suspend from tension wire through eyelets.
• Brighten up lengths of plain sheer fabric with appliqué: Use scraps of contrasting fabrics in cut-out shapes of stylized leaves or flowers, circles, or squares; or apply pockets of the main fabric to hold a changing exhibition of natural objects such as feathers, crystals, shells, dried leaves.
• The intricate work of timeless antique lace is best shown off as a flat panel rather than in gathered folds.
• Plan your nighttime lighting to highlight metallic threads in a sheer fabric to give you daytime and nighttime glamour (see 56).
• A system of sliding fabric panels on floor tracks or in the window frame can be opened or closed, depending on the need for privacy and light. A patterned, colored sheer with some weight is best, or you could use a combination of transparent and opaque fabric.

smooth and simple 61

As full-and-fancy curtain and drapery styles lose popularity, window shades and blinds have become increasingly stylish. They suit today's pared-down interior schemes and—let's be honest—save on expensive fabric.

• A roller shade is the most simple and useful of all, in stiffened or laminated fabric or in a firm fabric.

• Inverted roller shades ensure privacy without excluding all the light or view. The shade pulls up from a box fixed to the sill or outside the window recess.

• A Roman shade folds into flat pleats by means of cords. They look rather clean and minimal and come in all kinds of materials, from opaque or translucent fabrics to faux leather and suede.

• A Swedish shade, with the cord gliding through glass rings attached to the batten heading, works best with a naturally heavy fabric like linen.

• A reverse roll-up shade rolls up from the bottom by means of a pair of cords or straps. It suits lightweight fabrics best.

• A venetian blind is a sleek and modern solution for a window that doesn't require any dressing up. It can be made of stiffened fabric, wood, or perforated or solid aluminum.

• Vertical blinds suit floor-to-ceiling situations. They are made from synthetic polyester fabrics or plain or perforated aluminum.

• Inexpensive matchstick blinds consist of thin pieces of wood bound with thread, which usually roll up and are held in place with cords. They come in many colors, or can be natural or varnished.

• Bamboo blinds are light and textural with a natural finish.

• Paper shades are inexpensive. They work well in a Zen-look room and could be used to create zones in the bedroom in place of sliding screens.

62

alternative cover

There are situations where a different method of covering the window is needed, either because the shape of the window requires it or because your bedroom style suggests it. But you don't need an excuse; you might just like one of them!

• Plantation shutters are versatile and stylish. They look good on their own, or can be combined with curtains or draperies. The wooden slats open and close with a push-rod; another type has hinged flaps, allowing just the lower or upper half of the window to be shuttered.

• Sliding panels fixed to the ceiling are a neat solution to screening large areas of window—and for dividing the bedroom into zones (see 31, 32). When pulled by a draw rod, the linked panels slide behind one another.

• Hinged portière rods work well on tall, awkwardly placed windows. They allow panels of fabric to be swung open or closed.

• A freestanding screen (see 94) is an alternative for covering a bathroom or bedroom window, though it's unlikely to cover the entire window. If you have a fabric-covered screen, use two different fabrics, one on each side, for versatility.

63

combination treatments

A layered window treatment—combining draperies with sheer curtains, perhaps, or with a shade—can be both practical and decorative. It allows you to introduce different textures, patterns, and colors, or play down a busy drapery pattern with a cool, plain underlayer. On the practical side, an additional layer will give some privacy when draperies are open. And if the draperies are sheer, a blind or shade will screen out blackness at night.

doubled-up

A bedroom looks cozy and well dressed with panel draperies combined with ethereal sheer curtains. Use a special double traverse rod; or, if the sheer curtain is to remain static, hang it from an ordinary curtain rod.

loop the loop

If your window has a nice outline, preserve it while providing some degree of privacy. Make a luxurious fabric with a mitered border of a heavier fabric into a simple flat panel. To hold it back, hook it high from a loop on the opposite wall.

Add a roller shade, perhaps adding a border of the same fabric as the panel.

textural effects

Layered window treatments maximize the potential for big textural contrasts (see 44). Bamboo or woven wood blinds can be paired with a lustrous woven fabric or with a sleek delicate silk or taffeta edged with linen or burlap. Alternatively, the roles can be reversed combining draperies made of a coarse fabric, such as burlap or tweed, with delicate shades made of fine linen or another sheer material.

64
problem windows

It's ironic that a problem window often has an interesting shape and so really looks best without any adornment, but for practical reasons you may want to cover it up at night.

• If you have floor-to-ceiling panoramic windows, your options include sliding screens, vertical blinds, or accordion style shades.

• A bay or bow window is awkward to dress; the best solution is to use a series of blinds or shades. Alternatively, have curtains made to fit each window or hang panel draperies on either side.

• An arched window is such a bonus that it would be a shame to cover it, but you can make a Roman shade

with a semicircular plywood insert or use custom-made shutters.

• Options for a dormer window include a roller- or Roman shade, or hinged portière rods with short curtains that can be swung back against the interior window recess. Preferable to ordinary short curtains.

• Skylights pose a particular problem. There are specially designed Venetian or mini-blinds that draw along the window frame.

• Round or "ox-eye" windows are usually left uncovered, but for the sake of a good night's sleep, you could add a simple black-out curtain which can be drawn right back, leaving the window clear for daytime.

• A window that abuts a wall can't take a pair of draperies. A single drapery panel, blind, or shade will do.

hanging hardware

65

Draw draperies are normally hung from a traverse rod, which is fitted with cords and sliding rings. These come in a variety of styles. Give some thought to how the headings and method of hanging all work together, taking into account the weight and style of material, the decorative style of your bedroom, and the outlook and dimensions of your windows.

• Tension wire with rings and eyelets or with curtain clips is a neat, minimalist option for sheers and lightweight curtains.

• Fixed headings for draperies, curtains, and shades can be attached to a narrow batten or board fixed on or above the window frame.

• Traverse rods are usually made of metal or plastic. Double rods are available for hanging two pairs of draperies, one on top of the other, and for draperies plus a pleated valance. Some are designed for bay or bow windows. Although conventional traverse rods are slim and unobtrusive, you may wish to add a shaped or pleated valance, which will conceal the rod when the draperies are open.

• Wooden poles with finials come in a variety of sizes and are usually associated with draperies. They can be stained, painted, or even covered in the drapery material. Traverse rods that imitate this look are also available.

• Metal poles and rods are made in a variety of finishes such as iron, brass, and chrome.

• Lucite poles are particularly suitable for hanging delicate or sheer fabrics.

• Expansion rods are a neat solution for recessed windows or for any window where it's difficult to fix any other hardware. Although they can't support lined draperies, they're excellent for sheers and panels.

• An ever-increasing range of innovative window treatment hardware is available. You can now choose from a range of rings and clips, huge metal grommets, or simple cased or tab tops.

66

don't be floored by flooring

We have plenty of flooring options these days, don't we? Carpet remains enormously popular and comes in a fabulous range of updated classic styles and new-look designs. In addition we've got a dazzling choice of cutting-edge hard flooring materials. There has been a huge surge of interest in all kinds of hardwood and laminated floors to suit the leaner bedroom look; tiles and natural stone have always had a place in bedroom design, according to country and style; while carpeting is undergoing a major design revival. Old favorites such as linoleum and cork, which were once associated with the kitchen and bathroom, have been given a timely face-lift and now reappear in glamorous guise to floor the bedroom. Alternatives such as rubber, glass, and leather all have their part to play in the new-look bedroom, adding texture, color, and an unadulterated "wow" factor!

budget

Your choice of flooring will probably be influenced by the length of time you propose to stay in residence: You can't take a fixed floor with you but you could invest in a big rug, which is, of course, portable. Given that a new floor makes a huge visual impact, as well as an impact on your wallet, you will want to link what you spend to capital return, aesthetic effect, and practicality.

practicality

Above all, a floor needs to be practical for your individual situation and use. Think beyond the visual effect to wear-and-tear, staining, foot comfort, animals, and children. Can you combine your flooring with underfloor heating (see 16)? If you have pets in your bedroom consider the ease of cleaning and hygiene. If you have an in-bedroom bathtub or shower, you will want to choose a floor that is impervious to damp and water staining.

continuity

What other flooring do you have in the home? To help the overall visual flow, it's a good idea to have a link between the flooring of the bedroom and of the other rooms, particularly if there's an element of open-plan living. Likewise, consider continuing the same floor covering into the en-suite bathroom, if appropriate. Joins between rooms can be neatened with threshold strips.

style

Associate your flooring finish to your bedroom style, if possible. For example, dark or pale wood or bamboo floors work well in a minimalist oriental bedroom; pale or white-painted floorboards are associated with Swedish and East Coast looks; rubber, leather, and linoleum have an edgy look that suits urban loft living. Wall-to-wall carpet adds texture and, sometimes, pattern, while rugs can be specifically placed to add focal emphasis—and comfort underfoot—to certain areas.

space

When making decisions about flooring, consider its effect on the space: The horizontal surface can be manipulated by color, line, and pattern to visually alter a room's proportions: Floorboards, laid lengthwise, will elongate a room; a dark, thick-pile carpet will create a cozy cocoon; a brightly colored rug will draw attention to a particular area; textured rubber flooring gives a unique surface finish for a bedroom.

aesthetics

Be cautious! Can you live for years with the new must-have flooring choice? As necessary as it may seem now, today's faddish flooring material could be tomorrow's wallet-ache, especially if it clashes with the plans for the new bedroom you'll want in a couple of years' time.

environment

Certain types of flooring help alleviate allergies and prevent the accumulation of dust and bugs. Flooring that minimizes dust in the air and is easy to clean will help the allergy or asthma sufferer. Floors that don't throw up dust and other household detritus and are based on natural materials are thought to be best for the health, and these include linoleum, tiling, stone, and wood.

acoustics

Unfortunately, any hard flooring material will accentuate acoustic echo to some degree—and watch out for the creaking floorboard! For discretion, comfort, a change of texture, and to muffle some noise, include a few rugs.

weight

Most types of stone and all forms of marble are bulky and heavy. Since most timber floor joists are not strong enough to support a stone floor, this is something you must discuss with the fitters. It may be necessary to strengthen the joists if you're dead set on that stone floor.

en-suite bath

Bathroom fixtures should be installed after the linoleum or vinyl flooring is fitted. It's certainly possible to use wall-to-wall carpet (as long as it's not rubber-backed) in an en-suite bathroom; but although it may decoratively unite the bedroom and bathroom, it won't be as practical, long-lasting, or visually striking as floor tiles.

67 carpeting

There are now many handsome carpeting collections, so wall-to-wall carpeting is making something of a comeback. When choosing, first consider color, then texture, then whether you want solid-colored or patterned, and finally fiber and weave. Whatever you choose, be sure you can live with it, because carpeting is a long-term investment.

pile carpet

The most luxurious carpet is made entirely of wool, but because of its cost, wool is usually blended with nylon (the most popular fiber for carpets in the U.S.), which also provides extra durability. In a bedroom, durability is not such an issue, so if you can afford wool, go for it! To enhance the feeling of luxury, you might choose a cut pile, such as plush velvet, over a firmer loop pile, although the latter would be preferable for an adjoining bath. Berber carpet, with its dense looped pile in creams and grays, suits neutral color schemes.

natural fibers

All of these provide a useful neutral background, but some are not soft enough for bedrooms, and the only one suitable for a bath is rush matting.

Jute is not hard-wearing, but is softer than coir or sisal. Sisal is the strongest and hardest-wearing but is difficult to clean. Coir and seagrass are a bit prickly for bedroom use. If you like the appearance of natural fibers but without the disadvantages, consider a wool-mixture carpeting that imitates the look.

advantages of carpeting

• Softness
• Textural effects
• Creates a sense of spaciousness
• Introduces pattern and color
• Insulating qualities

disadvantages of carpeting

• Not good for allergy sufferers
• You can't take it with you when you move
• Might compromise design choices when you redecorate

68 wooden floors

Wooden flooring is the modern preference for many rooms. More comfortable underfoot than tiles or stone, it is good for creating a sense of space and coolness.

antique floorboards

These have a unique patina and character, but are very expensive. Your own boards may be suitable for restoration, but it's hard work.

solid wood flooring

This comes in a wide range of options. Ash, beech, and maple are the smoothest and palest; black walnut and merbau are dark and rich. High-density woods like oak are best for bathrooms. Treated with oil and wax, they are pretty water-tolerant. Cost is dictated by the width and length of the boards, and the type of wood.

hardwoods

In addition to the many native American hardwood species, there are dozens of exotic species. Make sure any hardwood you buy comes from a sustainable source. Teak, wenge, mahogany, and iroko are all endangered, but there are many eco-acceptable alternatives, including merbau—a lovely chestnut color—and dark-colored kwila—not stained by water so useful in a bathroom. Although expensive, parquet makes an attractive bedroom floor; but don't use it in wet areas, and have it expertly laid.

softwoods

These include fir, pine, and spruce. They must be finished with a sealer and polished. Sheets of sealed and varnished plywood (marine ply for a bathroom) are inexpensive and can be given a makeover with paint or stain.

laminate flooring

Cheaper than solid wood and easy to lay, but not so hard-wearing, laminated flooring can be damaged by high heels and can't be resanded. There are also cheap, nearly maintenance-free, strip floors made from high-pressure laminates. Laminated floors warp when wet, so aren't suitable for bathrooms.

bamboo

An excellent eco-friendly alternative to hardwood and less expensive than laminated flooring. Don't use in the bathroom, as it will swell when wet.

69

rugs and mats

Rugs come in a huge range of designs, colors, textures, and patterns and are great for zoning or acting as a focal point.

the rug choice

• Wool kilims and cotton dhurries are soft and come in rich, mellow colors and many different sizes
• Aubusson-style rugs are a perfect choice for an updated classic French or Italian-style bedroom
• Antique rugs are great for their character and soft coloring
• Rag rugs are inexpensive and look best on a pale or painted wooden floor
• Shag pile and flokati rugs are fun and are a real bedside treat-for-the-feet
• Animal-skin-effect rugs lend an exotic note to an earthy neutral color scheme or will associate handsomely with an updated Art Deco look
• Real animal hides add texture and "edge" to a hard floor
• Tatami mats and Goza mats suit a Zen-styled room
• Natural-fiber mats can be bought with lovely borders that soften their effect

70

other types of flooring

Sometimes carpets, wood, or rugs just don't make the grade. If you want bedroom flooring with attitude, consider one of these unusual options.

• Rubber tiles and sheeting are the flooring of the moment! They are anti-slip, anti-static, noise absorbing, warm underfoot, and resistant to burns. They can imitate stone and come in a range of smooth or textured effects in many different colors.
• Linoleum, in sheets or tiles and made from natural materials, has made a big comeback. Hygienic and eco-friendly, it comes in many designs and colors, including textured finishes such as "crocodile" and "tweed."
• Vinyl flooring comes in sheets or tiles that can be laid over almost any existing hard surface. It is not as long lasting or easy to maintain as linoleum, but is usually less expensive. Look for innovative vinyl-faced cork tiles printed with photographic images. They look great in a bathroom.
• Cork is back! Now in subtle new colors, it's durable, soft, impervious to water, a good insulator, and eco-friendly.

• Leather floor tiles are luxurious, warm, sensuous, and sound-insulating. However, they should be protected from direct sunlight, excessive heat, and sharp objects—including high heels!

• Concrete is an unusual bedroom flooring choice but is great if you want a raw and handsome look. It can be colored, skimmed with screed for a suede-like texture, or finished with a shiny resin coat.

• Consisting of marble chips set in a cement base and polished to a high sheen, terrazzo makes a handsome and non-slip floor.

• Tiles offer a wide choice, from unglazed terracotta, to glazed ceramic. They are good for continuity with an en-suite bath or wet room, but not kind to bare feet! Make sure you choose non-slip and check for weight (see 66) and subfloor requirements.

• Stone is another luxurious bedroom flooring option. Choose from cool limestone or marble for classic good looks (honed marble mosaic or tesserae are best for a bathroom as they are non-slip), granite or slate for more rugged appeal. Not all are as durable as you might think, though, so check before buying. And of course their weight and subfloor requirements are an issue.

• For the cutting-edge interior, how about glass floor tiles? They come in a range of colors and are available in a sandblasted non-slip finish.

give your floor a treat

time to strip

Although it's messy, stripping old floorboards gives you the look of plain boards without having to buy new. Once they're sanded, stain or paint, then seal with varnish.

top coat

All solid wood floors (see 68) should be sealed to protect them from damp and surface damage. Avoid polyurethane sealants because they are an irritant and will yellow the wood. Instead choose water-based acrylic or an organic treatment such as tung oil or citrus oil. These aren't as hard-wearing, so the floor will need regular waxing.

add an edge

Treat a plain wooden floor to a border such as a Greek key or checkerboard design, or use a stencil for more complexity.

carpet care

Professional on-site carpet cleaning will help restore your carpeting to its former glory. Professionals will comb the pile, power vacuum, machine clean, and hand-clean difficult areas. It really is worth the cost.

skin deep

Clean leather flooring with a lightly damp cloth or mop. Regular beeswax polishing will keep gaps filled in and improve luster.

You can be as choosy, opinionated, and selfish as you like in the privacy of your bedroom when it comes to deciding on your wall decoration. Whether you want an easy backdrop or a focused style, paint, wallpaper, and fabric are the main options, while tiles are most popular for an en-suite bath.

in character

Decorate your walls to underline your theme. For example, play up the decorative statement with a dramatic finish, such as a woven bamboo paper in an oriental-style room, or use subtly colored painted walls to create a neutral backdrop in a soothing bedroom full of textural detail.

versatility

Your wall treatment can refer to the style of bed and the way it is dressed, or it could coordinate with a curtain color. Because bedroom wall coverings don't have to be so hard-wearing, you could choose a hand-painted paper, suede-effect paint, or silk fabric without fear of damage from sticky fingers, muddy dogs, or sharp shopping bags!

disguise

Wallpaper or fabric disguises uneven or architecturally awkward walls. Cross-hung lining paper will smooth rough surfaces, and battens will hold fabric away from the walls. A broken paint finish will camouflage an uneven surface better than a solid one.

get focused

A single dynamically papered wall is enough to illustrate your stylistic direction without overwhelming a small bedroom. For example, convey an oriental flavor with a Chinese-style paper, or use a bold flower-and-stripe paper as a background for a pretty boudoir.

balance and proportion

Since the walls are the largest surface in the bedroom, how you decorate them is fundamental to creating the right atmosphere. Smart use of pattern, color, and texture on the walls can make the room look larger or smaller and give visual focus, but balance between these elements is vital to provide a tranquil environment. And remember, daylight has a great effect on how we see color and texture, but in the bedroom, nighttime lighting is by far the more important influence.

architectural details

Chair rails and panels can be a boon or a bore. A high-ceilinged bedroom can accommodate the horizontal divide that a chair rail creates, but in most bedrooms a rail simply creates bad proportions and affects the visual flow. If the feature is genuine, it will almost certainly look right and, like other genuine architectural features, should be treasured and enhanced.

combination finishes

With such a large area to play with, walls offer many opportunities for exciting

combinations. For greatest impact, try to exaggerate the textural differences—a large patterned wallpaper with sleek satin-varnished paint finish; a natural grass-fiber paper with one lacquer-effect-painted wall; "suede" walls with quilted silk wall panels.

and not forgetting the ceiling

Until the 1920s, the ceiling was considered part of the decorative playground, but it has since been largely ignored. Instead of painting it plain old white, why not adorn it with another color, with stenciling, geometric shapes, or a mural? After all, you spend a third of your life facing the ceiling!

bed and bath links

Create continuity and a feeling of spaciousness between the bedroom and an en-suite bath by using a single walling material in a neutral color for the two rooms. Or link the bathroom walls and those of the bedroom following the style of decoration of the bedroom. For instance, use high-gloss tiles and chrome with an updated Art Deco theme, color-washed tongue-and-groove paneling for the seaside look, or handmade tiles, inlaid mirror, and earthy pigment colors to accompany a Moroccan-inspired bedroom.

trying times

Always try out samples of paint or wallpaper on large pieces of board propped up against the different walls of the bedroom to see how light affects them. Bear in mind, too, the effect that electric light (see Balance and Proportion) will have.

73

paint

Paint is inexpensive and versatile. No wonder it's such a popular finish.

paint basics

Matte water-based paint is the easiest, quickest and most inexpensive method of decorating walls and ceilings. Eggshell and satin finishes are good for surfaces that are vulnerable to marking, for painting radiators, or for adding subtle contrast.

eco

Water- or acrylic-based alternatives to solvent-based paints are eco-friendly, better for allergies, skin, and nose—and dry quicker!

color match

Most paint colors can be found commercially, but for an inimitable deep and lustrous finish, you can create your own color using powder pigments or tinting colors in an acrylic base, and apply several coats. Finish with an appropriate varnish.

textural effects

Besides the ubiquitous latex flat, there are more unusual paints that will give textural interest to bedroom walls. Buttermilk paint has a lovely soft finish, well suited to traditional rooms. For extra luxury, suede-effect paint is available from specialist dealers; have it applied by a professional decorator.

lacquer

Lacquer paint in red or black suits an oriental bedroom. It needs a completely smooth surface, so is best applied to a small area—a single wall or wardrobe front.

metallic

Metallics used for contrasting detail add a touch of glamour to a bedroom. Glittery and opalescent paints, on top of water-based paint or for added detail, are an option.

colorwash

Achieve a soft, cloudy effect with tinted colorwashes using either a polyvinyl "carrier" or diluted water-based paint. This finish will need a varnish topcoat.

74

wood

Wood has been used for paneling interior walls for centuries, but except in countries where it grows plentifully, it is no longer common, especially not for bedrooms. However, it adds warmth and texture and can make a valuable contribution to bedroom and bath walls. As with wooden flooring, make sure you buy wood from a sustainable source (see 68).

paneling

This should be custom made and expertly fitted. Leave it unpainted for a handsomely masculine bedroom; paint it cream or soft green for an Arts and Crafts look; or give it a distressed finish in blue green or dusty pink for an 18th-century feel.

tongue-and-groove

This is paneling's country cousin, conjuring up seaside and rustic bedrooms. Use pale colors to keep the effect light: paint or colorwash in the bedroom, paint and varnish in the en-suite bath.

rough lumber

For a rustic country cabin look or for texture in a large open-plan bedroom, use old scaffolding planks or railway ties cut into thin planks.

plywood

An economical alternative to solid hardwood, plywood can be used to simulate paneling if you paint lines on it. The best quality, veneer-core plywood, consists of seven thin layers of hardwood and is strong and lightweight.

bamboo

With its ridged and glossy texture, bamboo makes a dramatic wall cladding, but it is best confined to a single wall. It is also available as woven wall tiles.

special treatment

If wood seems too heavy, lighten its effect and emphasize the grain with a colorwash, or "lime" it using a special paste. The result is a weathered, aged look. Particleboard can be painted or "grained" to simulate planking or paneling. A wall-to-wall "wood" closet system could be created in this way, too.

stone, brick, plaster, and concrete

Using these wall finishes takes courage and probably a pretty unique bedroom. But they can work well combined with more usual wall treatments. It's best to think extremes—a rough stone wall behind a velvet headboard, a concrete half-wall screening off a glass-and-chrome shower unit, a reclaimed brick wall showing off a gallery of colorful pictures in old gilt frames.

stone

• Stone is textural, cool, and heavy and amplifies sound.

• If you have stone walls, they can be exposed to make a feature wall in the bedroom. In an en-suite bath or shower area, they give the feeling that you are bathing outdoors.

• Limestone and slate can be used on walls and floors, so can bring a sense of unity to an en-suite bath or wet room. Marble's opulent image has detracted somewhat from its merits recently, but it is worth considering for its beautiful patterning and color for bathroom walls. It is slippery when wet, so not recommended for the floor.

brick

• Brick can suit either a rustic or a contemporary bedroom.

• It comes in a variety of natural shades, which you'll have to consider carefully when choosing other colors to go with it in the bedroom

• Interior brick should be treated with sealant to prevent dusting; it can also be colored with masonry paint.

plaster

• Most walls are finished with plaster or Sheetrock, so why not make this into a decorative asset? It gives a softly textured, informal wall finish and works very well on uneven walls.

• Color pigments may be worked into the dry plaster mix or rubbed into the wall surface. Unpainted plaster must be sealed to stop it from dusting. It can be waxed and polished for a deep, luminous finish.

• Unfinished plaster should not be used in damp areas, but waterproofed and sound-insulating Sheetrock is available.

concrete

• Concrete's utilitarian appeal isn't for everyone's bedroom, but you could consider using it as a room divider if your bedroom is big enough.

• In an en-suite bath, concrete provides a bold contrast to polished, shiny chrome and porcelain.

76 wallpaper

Because patterned walls have been out of fashion for a while, wallpaper has taken a back seat, but if you want to convey a specific decorative image in your bedroom, then wallpaper is the preferred choice. You might choose a warm-colored, dense pattern to create a cocooning environment, a themed design to reflect the style of the room—floral, Provençal, geometric retro—or an extravagantly expensive paper to make a fabulous stand-alone statement. If adding texture is your main aim, go for imitation rice paper or parchment for a Zen den, natural fiber papers as a subtle backdrop to a neutral look, or imitation suede embossed with a geometric pattern for the retro look.

Innovative wallpapers include those with metallic threads or overlaid abstract metallic shapes. They look stunning under subtle nighttime lighting, which is all-important to a bedroom. Papers for en-suite bath walls are more limited because they have to have a vinyl finish to protect them from moisture, but they make a worthy alternative to tiles, where economy is a major consideration.

practical pointers

• Make sure you take the repeat of a pattern into account when calculating wallpaper quantities. This is especially important with a large design.

• Always look at a picture of the wallpaper hung in situ; it may have an unexpected striped, diagonal, curved, or wavy pattern.

• If the walls are uneven or you're using a delicate wallpaper, first line the walls using plain paper (available from specialist dealers) hung horizontally. You can also use lining paper on the ceiling.

• To make a room appear longer, instead of painting horizontal stripes, you could use a broad-striped paper hung horizontally—it's easier than trying to paint straight lines!

• Awkward shapes and angles in a room can be disguised by using a paper with a loose, unstructured pattern on all the surfaces, including the ceiling.

• If you like the idea of fabric on the walls, look for paper-backed fabric. This is much easier to apply than battens plus fabric.

• Use panels of paper to freshen up cabinet doors. Frame them with beading and insert a pretty wallpaper panel, or cover them completely with wallpaper if you want them to "disappear."

there is an alternative
other wall coverings

Even if you are using wallpaper and paint as the main wall treatments in your bedroom, there might be situations where you want to introduce a change of texture, manipulate the light, or use a single wall area in an interesting way. Some of these alternatives can be used as a means of refreshing an existing theme or giving your new style an unexpected dimension.

glass

There are glass finishes to suit every purpose—sandblasted, etched, printed, textured, toughened, wired, and laminated—and in colors to suit every color scheme. Glass blocks allow the passage of light and are a fashionable choice, either as a partition in the bath or as a dividing wall between bedroom and wet room.

mirror

A mirrored wall will dramatically enlarge the sense of space in a small bathroom; however, it needs to be kept spotless to look good! In the bedroom, where large areas of mirror can be intimidating, it's best used in panels, or divided with beading or trellis. You might front a wall of built-in closets with mirror.

fabric

For loose draperies, hang supple fabric from hooks or brackets so that it falls in swags against the wall, looping from hook to hook. For a tented effect use a striped fabric or light canvas and "tent" the ceiling too. For ultimate cocooning, fix battens to the walls and staple on lengths of fabric, finishing the joins with braid, gimp, or ribbon.

oddball paper

Tissue paper, wrapping paper, and rice paper all make interesting alternative wall coverings. The wall beneath will show through, so paint it an appropriate color. Protect the paper with varnish or a tinted wash. Use metallic leaf, too, for a unique burnished tile effect.

77

bedtime at last

A bed is a major investment and is often the centerpiece for your bedroom style. Some people choose a bed for its looks, while others choose one they hope will ease their back pain. If your bedroom has limited storage space, you might be drawn to a bed with storage potential, or you may decide that your top priority is a really huge bed. But whatever style choice you go for, the first priority is to buy the best mattress you can afford (see 80). Choosing the frame is the next step. The range of prices, styles, and qualities of beds and mattresses is enormous. It's enough to make you want to lie down!

did you know?

Did you know that you spend one-third of your life in bed and that you should replace your mattress every 10 years?

10 ideas

headboards

Most people like a headboard for comfort and to protect the wall behind the bed. You can buy your bed complete with a headboard, or choose a separate one. A traditional upholstered headboard can be finished to match or contrast with your bed dressing or draperies. Modern versions are sometimes just made of wood or consist of a flat, padded surface in a material such as faux suede, moleskin, or even leather. If you are thinking of having a headboard made, order the biggest you can accommodate—bigger is almost always better.

size matters

Antique beds are often shorter and a different width from a modern standard bed. However, a specialized manufacturer can produce a mattress made to exactly the right dimensions—but this will obviously cost more than a mass-produced one. If you're buying an antique bed, check that the base of the bed is strong and complete, too!

futons

A futon mattress is ideal for a Zen-style bedroom, but because it lies close to the ground, dust and drafts can be a problem.

sofa beds

Try it out before buying it; the "sofa" part can be deceptively commodious and comfortable compared to the "bed" part! An easily adapted futon-style sofa bed makes a sleek modern alternative.

daybeds

A daybed with scrolled or comfortably upholstered ends is an elegant option for single occupancy in a studio or loft room where space is limited. Some have a sliding frame underneath containing a mattress so they turn into a double bed when required (see 93).

well adjusted

Adjustable beds are either manually or electrically operated and give you the option of individualized sitting and sleeping positions. They come with either flexible laminated slats or fully upholstered sections with special mattresses. The ultimate luxury bed has a fully electronically adjustable system, including integrated heating and airing facilities!

space savers

Raising your bed on a platform gives the illusion of more space and offers the potential for extra storage underneath, too. Always invest in a good-quality innerspring mattress for comfort. For occasional guests, a twin bed with another bed underneath that is jacked up to the same height is an option (see 35); or for the ultimate in space saving, investigate a wall bed. This is a complete unit with a spring and hinge mechanism that can be recessed into the wall and lowered into position when required.

kids' beds

If the children are old enough, bunk beds are an obvious space saver and fun too! Avoid claustrophobia by providing good lighting and plenty of headroom. For coziness, you could surround the beds with curtains or roll-up shades. A bed built into a

closet is another fun idea, and space saving too, while a truckle bed, which pulls out from beneath another bed, is perfectly adequate for sleepovers and keeps little cherub friends close and cozy.

underbed storage

Many beds have the option of underbed storage. You can buy or order a bed with drawers in the base—either a large drawer at the foot end, a pair of drawers on each side, or four drawers of varying size. Many low-line modern beds also have underbed storage drawers, while a high bedstead has plenty of space that can be filled with boxes, baskets, zippered cases, or drawers on wheels (see 79, 86).

bed styles

A bed will usually dominate a bedroom, so think before you buy a French antique bed or an ultra-modern chrome bed frame. It will govern the decorations long after you have grown tired of it!

contemporary wood

Modern wooden bed frames are often on slim, tapered legs or on a low-rise platform, and they sometimes come with a simple headboard or with integral bedside tables. They are ideal for the uncluttered loft or Zen-style bedroom. For luxury and contrast, look for an oversized headboard in tactile leather, suede, woven bamboo, or rattan.

tubular steel

Bed frames of robust tubular steel with an upholstered or wooden headboard make an interesting combination and suit a clean-cut urban bedroom.

ironwork

A modern take on traditional Italian and Provençal beds, contemporary ironwork beds look more streamlined but still echo the sleek curves of the original.

box spring and mattress

Sometimes called a Hollywood bed, this simple combination includes a headboard but no footboard—good for showing off a flowing bedspread or quilt. It lies close to the floor, but some models offer storage space in the form of drawers in the box spring base.

four-poster

The traditional four-poster may seem heavy for today's bedrooms but if you have one, dress it to make the most of it. Modern four-posters are lighter in style, with simple uprights. They may be hung with draperies or stay uncurtained. Most are of wood, but some have square-sectioned metal frames.

lit bateau

The lit bateau, or sleigh bed, with its solid wood base and scrolled ends, is a classic French design of the early 19th century. It gets its name from its shape. There are classic and modern interpretations.

antique beds

Antique beds can have either a metal or a wood—often carved—frame. Some, typically French, versions have canework panels in the head- and footboards, while another has a high, shaped head- and footboard in carved and upholstered wood.

80 mattress matters

However glamorous your bed, the mattress is more important. Don't test it just by bouncing up and down on the edge—spend time in the store lying on it in your usual sleeping and reading positions.

sizes

U.S. bed sizes: twin: 38" x 75"; full: 53" x 75"; queen: 60" x 80"; king: 76" x 80".
Before you buy, check the size of doorways and stairways to make sure the bed will fit! If you want a king-size bed but can't get it through the door, buy two twins and a king-size mattress.

innerspring construction

The best mattresses contain coiled springs, but there is an enormous range in their quality. Some of the relevant factors are the number of coils, the way they are formed and positioned, and the gauge, or thickness, of the wire used. The thickness and quality of the padding are other contributing factors.

number of coils

The more coils a mattress contains, the better it will conform to your body. A double, or full-size, mattress should contain at least 300 coils, a queen size about 400, and a king size about 480.

coil construction

A continuous coil system consists of a single strand of wire and offers firm support. Other systems use separate coils, which may be knotted together at the top, left unknotted, or enclosed individually in cloth or plastic pockets.

wire gauge

As a general rule, the thicker the wire gauge, the better the quality. A 13-gauge wire is generally used in the better mattresses, though a finer wire, such as 18-gauge, may be used where the coil count is very high.

foam

A good-quality foam mattress should have a high density. The newest are made of visco-elastic foam that molds itself to the shape of any object or weight but returns to its original state when the weight is removed. A foam mattress is used with a slatted base.

latex

A good choice for allergy sufferers, it is usually sold with a slatted base but can also be bought with a deep-sprung box spring.

made-to-order

You can have a mattress made to your requirements.

single solution

If you and your partner are of very different weights, or prefer different degrees of firmness in a bed, consider buying two twin beds and pushing them together (as is done in some small hotel rooms in Europe). This gives you, in effect, a king-size bed, and you can dress it accordingly.

water bed

Although these may conjure up an image of lasciviousness, they are extremely good for poor circulation, bad backs, and allergy sufferers.

headboard ideas to suit all tastes

A headboard or decorative backdrop provides
a starting point for the bed arrangement and adds another
element of vertical decoration.

fabric panel

A length of beautiful fabric (see 47) hung behind the
bed gives the illusion and visual definition of a
headboard. Choose a heavy fabric with a non-
directional pattern so you can hang it horizontzally.
Insert a thin batten into a pocketed heading at the top
and attach it with rings to hidden hooks on the wall
above the bed. Another batten or weights in a hem at
the bottom will keep it hanging straight.

shaggy story

Make an impact with a headboard made from
sheepskin or a flokati rug hung behind the bed or
used to upholster a plywood template. Deliciously soft
and slightly eccentric!

reclaimed

A bit of lateral thinking will suggest some interesting
"alternative" headboards such as carved antique
doors, fretwork screens, sanded and painted
scaffolding planks, and bamboo fencing material.

82
a cut above
draperies and hangings

You don't have to have a four-poster to dress up your bed with hangings.

simplicity itself
Twist and drape a length of lightweight or sheer fabric over a large hook in the ceiling or a bracket on the wall above the bed.

canopy
Four small hooks fixed to the ceiling above the bed can hold lengths of doweling parallel with the bed's front edge. Simply drape fabric over the doweling, allowing the fabric to fall over the front one to form a valance and over the back one to hang down the wall behind the bed.

pole attachments
A simple drapery can be made using two or three poles and finials extending from the wall to hold a throw-over length of material. If you use three poles, center the middle one high over the bed to create a triangular, rather than rectangular, shape. Either go for a light and airy effect with a gossamer fabric or give the drapery weight with a contrast lining and border or trimming.

tester
A tester is a canopy attached to the wall or ceiling above the bed. For a contemporary look, simply staple or tack a lightweight fabric to the ceiling/wall. A corona has a semicircular frame. Again, the fabric can be stapled or tacked on, but to get even pleating, sew on heading tape first. A corona works especially well hanging over a daybed.

alternative dressing
For an updated version of bed draperies on a contemporary four-poster, use soft roll-up fabric shades or matchstick or bamboo

slatted blinds fixed to the top cross-bars. If you want full curtains, try unusual fabrics such as linen, burlap, taffeta, or gingham.

keeping track
Suspend draperies from ceiling-mounted poles or from traverse rods lined up with the outline of the bed. A four-poster look without the posts!

83 all dressed up

It's important to keep your style perspective focused when it comes to dressing the bed; it's all too easy to throw on any old sheets or bedspreads and ruin your carefully thought-out look. But first you have to make some basic choices.

the basics

• A well-tailored bed needs sheets and blankets: Egyptian cotton sheets are top quality and look and feel crisp and cool, while Irish linen has an inimitable look and softness. Harder work than throwing over the comforter, but blankets in lambswool or ultra-luxurious mohair or cashmere edged with satin offer layers of warmth and tactile pleasure.

• There is always a tussle between the merits of sheets and blankets versus comforters. If you choose a comforter look for quality; pocket-stitched goose down is top quality, followed by feather and down and then hollow fiber.

• The best-quality pillows are goose down, followed by duck down and duck feather. There are various grades of synthetic fillings, sizes, and shapes.

the decoration

• A classic quilt offers a warm and comforting top layer for blankets and mixes well with a contemporary style. Today's versions are likely to be made from solid-colored, rich fabrics.

• A bedspread should reflect the decorations of your bedroom. Double-sided versions offer an alternative when they are turned back on the bed or a completely different look when you reverse them.

• A throw or runner adds a touch of modern glamour to a bed.

• When it comes to cushions, mix different shapes and textures, but limit the pattern or the bed will look busy rather than inviting. Trimmed and tasseled bolster shapes suit antique French beds, but the tailored version looks at home on a contemporary bed.

earthy and natural
• linen, burlap, calico, cotton, wool

tailored and masculine
• herringbone, tweeds, wide-wale corduroy, denim

minimal zen
• printed blue-and-white or black-and-white cotton, a touch of silk

boudoir
• silky textures, printed florals

scandinavian
• simple checked, plaid, or striped cotton

storage basics

Keeping the bedroom clean and clutter-free will help maintain an organized, harmonious environment, which is fundamental for relaxing and sleeping. The arrangement of bedroom storage needs careful planning, so the storage units are chosen for accessibility and efficient use of space. So many different items need to be stored in a bedroom that the result is bound to be a mixture of hanging, drawer, and shelf space, in varying proportions. You will also need to consider the size of the storage units and the space allotted to them; and apart from all this, you will have to think about relating your storage to your bedroom style and budget.

10 ideas

distribution

Making sure that things are easy to put away and retrieve is vital. It will mean you actually use your storage properly. Allocating space for specific items will help a lot.

suits you?

Choose your storage to suit your lifestyle. If you're a suit person, your closet space should be designed with suits and shirts in mind, but if you're a sporty person or have a penchant for expensive underwear, you will probably need more shelf and drawer space.

sharing

If you share your bedroom with someone, you'll also have to share the storage space. This requires some give and take, so allocate space according to need, and stick to it.

making a fresh start

It's cathartic to sort through your stuff and get rid of what you don't need, and it's essential when planning your bedroom storage. It's easy to find any number of reasons why you must hang on to a certain item of clothing, but if you haven't worn it for more than two years, now is the time to say goodbye!

keep it moving

Work out how frequently you need to access something, as in "rarely," "sometimes," or "often," and store your possessions accordingly. Just because you have a shoe rack doesn't mean next winter's boots have to occupy valuable space there all the time, so keep things moving.

walk in

If you are lucky enough to be planning a new en-suite bathroom, build a false wall and you could have a walk-in closet area between the two rooms. If there is little room to open doors, use sliding panels, a neat curtain, or a roller shade instead (see 31, 33).

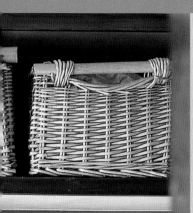

room to grow

Try to keep some flexibility in your storage arrangements for expansion, change of use, or different priorities. Perhaps you could choose a modular system, which can be added to when necessary, or "building-block" open storage units whose shelf arrangements can be changed as your storage needs change.

showing off

Are you amazingly tidy, have stunning, color co-ordinated clothes, and iron like a god/goddess? If so, you might opt for open storage or state-of-the-art closets with interior lighting so your clothes will be on display—but you'll also need a chest of drawers for those little things that aren't perhaps so decorative!

aesthetically pleasing

Exchange those old wire hangers for an assortment of wooden ones for skirts, slacks, and shirts; line drawers with quality paper, scented if you like—and change it seasonally—and install, and use, shoe racks.

a good finish

• Hardwood (see 74): cherry, stained oak, and walnut for a cozy, dark effect; light oak, maple, ash, beech for a lighter contemporary look
• Softwoods (see 74): waxed and polished or painted; plywood; veneers
• Bamboo (see 74): Textural, aesthetic, and original; use either as split lengths or woven "tiles"
• Glass (see 77): etched or frosted; crisp and contemporary; offers a lighter finish than wood for an entire wall of

wardrobes, with the possibility of subtle interior lighting
• Polypropylene: opaque panels are most effective, especially with interior lighting
• Mirror: reflects light, changes a room's perspective, and gives you a chance to preen
• Fabric (see 47, 52): texture related to room's design; use in pleated or flat panels behind glass, wire, doweling, trellis, or fretwork
• Painted particleboard (see 73): Easy to relate to a room's decoration and change and touch-up when necessary
• Wallpaper (see 76): use as built-in closet camouflage, either all over or as panels on the doors

freestanding or built-in?

If you've embraced a pared-down lifestyle, you may be able to stow all your clothes and accessories in a single closet and a chest of drawers. But if you're like most of us, you've acquired a lot more than these will contain—unless your closet is of the commodious walk-in variety. In planning more storage space, you have two basic choices: built in or freestanding.

three freestanding options

1 • Ready-to-assemble, or RTA: At the economy end of the freestanding storage options are wardrobes and armoires that you assemble yourself. These come in a huge range of styles—some designed mainly for clothes, with hanging rails and/or drawers, and some for other items, such as TV and audio equipment. The choice of finishes and decorative styles is huge, and quality, of course, varies considerably.

2 • Ready-made: More convenient, time-saving, and stress-free, ready-assembled storage will probably be more strongly constructed.

3 • Antique: However handsome it looks, an antique wardrobe or armoire is usually inadequately fitted inside for contemporary storage requirements, but you could get a carpenter to adapt it for your needs. Check before you buy that the depth is adequate for a modern hanger if you're using it for clothing.

advantages
• Flexible—easy to add to, adapt for changing needs, or move around
• You can take it with you when you move

disadvantages
• Less easy to create a coordinated look
• Less efficient use of space
• Less versatile interior space
• Limited range of materials

room divider

In a large bedroom or a studio apartment, a freestanding shelf and/or cabinet system can also serve as a room divider. Buy an off-the-rail version or have one custom-built. It can either be static or fitted with sturdy, lockable wheels.

two built-in options

1 • Closet organizers: Intended mainly for use inside existing closets, these modular units can be combined in all sorts of ways and will greatly increase the amount of storage space within a closet. Some can be fitted with doors and used in the bedroom itself.

2 • Custom made: Offers the chance for storage that is completely in tune with your bedroom style and storage needs. Choose a carpenter whose work you have seen and like and who can help you make the most of the available space—for example those awkward-shaped places around the bed and the bath fixtures. Think beyond standard finishes and details so your storage is as personal and stylish as possible.

advantages

- Looks sleek and coordinated
- Efficient use of space
- Good selling point
- Can be custom-built to suit a particular decorative style and to accommodate architectural elements such as a crown molding and baseboards
- Interior fittings can be custom-built to suit personal requirements

disadvantages

- Not for the impatient
- If custom-made, more costly than freestanding
- Lack of flexibility if your needs change
- Requires a certain level of skill if you do it yourself; otherwise, cost of professional installation
- You can't take it with you when you move

86 open shelves

Open shelves are versatile and should be chosen to blend with your bedroom's décor. You will need various sizes and widths to accommodate a mixture of items, but whatever their use, choose the same style throughout for a unified look. And because it's all too easy to overcrowd shelves, you'll need to be rigorous in keeping them tidy; otherwise the effect will be ruined.

shelving to suit

Relate the style, size, and construction of your shelving to your decorative look: slim, floating shelves for a minimalist feel; ornate rococo style for the boudoir; bamboo and rope for the Zen interior.

in proportion

It's important to "balance" the look of the shelving to help the decorative flow. The best arrangement is in blocks, either vertical, pyramid-shaped, or stepped. And try to position it near other furniture. In isolation on the wall, shelving looks bulky.

go with the flow

If you have fixed ceiling-to-floor shelving units, make sure their design continues the line of architectural features such as baseboards and crown moldings.

let there be light

To add glamour to your shelving and reflect the light, "line" the back of open shelves with mirror; alternatively edge them with a lip deep enough to conceal any downlights.

storage as display

Use shelving to hold storage boxes made of wicker, rattan, bamboo, steel, fabric, or covered with paper. Chosen to complement your room style, these can be decorative in their own right.

en-suite bath

If you have a suitable window in your en-suite bath, why not fix sturdy glass or mirrored shelves across it to hold toiletries, flowers, and candles?

87

clothes and shoes

In an ideal world, all our clothes and shoes would exactly fit into the bedroom closet and chest of drawers in a miraculous and permanently tidy manner. Our ironing, folding, and color-coordinating skills would be supreme, and our rigorous annual review would ensure seamless seasonal changeovers. But in reality, we have to strive to create a workable clothes storage system, aided and abetted by some creative thinking and discipline!

hanging clothes

Divide hanging space into sections for skirts, dresses, shirts, and slacks according to length. This saves space. Item-specific hangers are very useful.

folded clothes

Correctly folded garments take up less space. Chests of drawers or tallboys are one option for folded clothes, stacking boxes or baskets on wall-mounted brackets are others.

shoes

Shoe racks, drawers, cubbyholes, and hanging holders will keep pairs of shoes united. Boots can be hung from clips on hangers or stuffed with boot trees. If you use hanging shoe bags, identify their contents with luggage labels, and if shoe boxes are your thing, use a glued-on photo.

socks and pantyhose

Shoe bags and small laundry bags are great for storing socks and pantyhose.

belts and ties

If you don't mind having them on view, you could use an antique towel rail or a decorative ladder. Otherwise, hang them inside closet doors or on a hanging rack.

scarves 'n' shawls

Pretty enough to be seen, you could make a feature by draping them over the back of a chair or hanging them from a tabletop or floor-standing mirror.

hats

Hats are awkward to store and take up a lot of space. The best solution is traditional hatboxes, covered in a pretty paper and left on view.

by the bed

The sort of things you may want by your bed at night include a light, phone, alarm clock, books and magazines, notepad and pen, reading glasses, water and drinking glass, tissues, maybe flowers, and a little photo or two—and those are just the things you see! How you deal with bedside storage will depend on how much room and stuff you have and the style of your bedroom.

classic

A classic bedside table with a shelf underneath and a cabinet below is ideal. You can put the essentials on top, the often-needed on the shelf and the can't-shows in the cabinet!

antique

Search antique shops or salesrooms for an old nightstand with a cabinet that used to hold the chamber pot. They look good in a traditional bedroom and are practical, too. Alternatively, you might find an ornate rococo-style side table that would suit a boudoir look.

freewheeling

A good solution to bedside storage is to choose a hospital-style storage unit on wheels. It will give your room a definite aesthetic!

built-in

Some bed frames have integral tables, shelves, or drawers. They look streamlined but aren't very roomy.

in the wall

A recessed shelf can be built into the wall behind the bed or even into a wide, purpose-built headboard. You could have downlights wired into it if you don't want wall lights.

space savers

doors and walls

There's often space above the door to include a cabinet, and don't forget the wall above the bed. Back-of-door hooks and wall hooks are useful, and you can fill corners with shelves or a wardrobe.

under the bed

A box spring base or a contemporary design with drawers underneath (see 78) offers useful storage, as does a classic high bedstead (see 78) or a bed on a deep platform (see 32, 33).

coat stand

A coat stand, complete with good-looking hangers, doesn't take up much room and is especially useful for guest rooms (see 35).

windows

If you have a recessed or bay window or an alcove, build in a window seat or bench with storage underneath—either drawers or cabinets. Or place a deep ottoman with storage space in this location.

90 solutions for small things

Small items like cosmetics, makeup, jewelry, loose change, buttons, pills, business cards, cufflinks, pens, and sunglasses can be a real nuisance to keep safely stored yet readily accessible. Some of the following receptacles will tame and contain them.

boxes

In cardboard, wood, lacquer, leather, Lucite, or metallic finish—choose a collection of one type to suit your bedroom style. And remember that hatboxes aren't just for hats. Cover them to suit—floral or toile paper for a girly boudoir, geometric abstracts for fifties retro—and leave them on show.

baskets

Suiting a bedroom with a country or ethnic edge, woven baskets of all kinds add texture and convenience.

bags

Stow small treasures and makeup in decorative handbags displayed on a shelf or pegs, or make small bags in a fabric to coordinate with your room.

suitcases and hampers

Old leather and canvas cases or new metal ones are great for underwear, socks, and toiletries in an urban loft-style or safari-look bedroom. Hampers are practical for the bedroom and the en-suite bath for holding spare bedding, towels, lightbulbs, and toilet paper. Stack these in decreasing sizes to save room.

bowls and pots

Glass, ceramic, wood, lacquer, or wirework bowls or a row of terracotta, metal, or ceramic flowerpots can be used for makeup, change, jewelry, and other odds and ends.

mugs and glasses, cups and saucers

Colorful and decorative, these can be used to hold small cosmetic items, pens, and sunglasses. Pretty antique cups and saucers are inexpensive and are perfect for earrings, cufflinks, and loose change.

help! what do I do with my entertainment center?

91

Entertainment equipment has really come out of the closet. State-of-the-art technology has created audio and TV systems that are designed to be seen. But, however beautiful the system, you won't want to see a tangle of wires and cords, so make sure they are well concealed. You obviously need the system to be in the best possible place for listening, viewing, and operating (see 18), and, as we all know, size does matter in the bedroom so select a system whose size suits your space. If you feel that the whole thing interferes with your bedroom style, hide it behind a sliding screen or in a closet, or choose the smaller-is-less-of-an-eyeful option.

finishing touches

Before turning to the fine detailing, which will stamp the bedroom with your personal style, there are still some practical questions to be answered and some decisions to be made. For example, what will you use as a dressing table, and where will you sit? Where will you perch to put your shoes on? Is a separate desk necessary? Will you want somewhere comfortable to feed your baby or read a book? Hopefully, if your answers mean you have to fit more furniture into the room, you'll have enough space to do so. Otherwise, some creative thinking will be needed, and that desk will have to double up as a makeup area, or that armchair will need to incorporate some useful storage.

sitting and lounging

Most bedrooms need one practical chair. If you have room for an armchair, it's a bonus, while a sofa or chaise longue is a real luxury.

essential seating

Choose a stylish, modern stool or a dainty cane or gilt chair to tuck under a dressing table. An upholstered ottoman can also provide storage space.

Desk chairs come streamlined in pale wood or retro in stained, molded plywood, and metal. Alternatively, use a folding chair that you bring out when necessary.

lounge lizard

Delicate upholstery fabric in the bedroom is usually acceptable because it's not subject to much wear and tear, but slipcovers are often more practical. If you have the luxury of two sets you can rotate them seasonally.

Sensuous and luxurious, a leather sofa or chair will outlive many styles and fashions. It can look quite masculine, so you may want to soften its appearance with throws and cushions.

Chaises longues come in traditional or modern styles—velvet-covered and serpentine, or molded shapes covered with leather or suede.

Canvas director's chairs or Lucite chairs are not usually associated with a bedroom, but they can work well. The non-color and simple contours of Lucite allow it to mix with antique or modern ingredients. Lloyd Loom furniture is another bedroom option—but more for perching on than serious lounging.

You could also consider cane, wicker, rattan, and bamboo, as well as planter's style chairs, with their woven cane backs and seats. All these are light in style and will add a textural dimension. They are also versatile, mixing well with antique or modern furniture and with oriental or colonial bedrooms.

tables and screens

94

A dressing table is an essential piece of bedroom furniture, especially if you don't have an en-suite bathroom, but you will need to have the luxury of space if you hope to include a writing table as well! If you're not meticulously tidy, a screen will help to hide a multitude of sins.

five dressing table options

1 • Classic skirted kidney-shaped table for an opulent boudoir

2 • Rectangular with a "tablecloth" top and skirt trimmed with crystal droplets

3 • Bevel-mirrored kneehole table for an updated Art Deco bedroom

4 • Painted to suit the room's color scheme

5 • Slim-profile console table

writing table

It's best to keep a bedroom writing table small—unless, of course, your bedroom doubles as a study (see 34). A small one won't attract clutter or overwhelm the room. Look for the simplest design—slim-legged and narrow-topped in glass and steel, wood and paint or lacquer and inlay.

screens

A screen provides privacy (see 63, 64), zones different areas of the room, and can even act as a freestanding headboard. It also adds an unusual vertical dimension.

• Indian, Moroccan, African, or oriental fretwork is very decorative and allows some light to filter through.

• There are many well-finished contemporary designs in solid wood, or you might find an old paneled screen. You could also have a screen made in timber, plywood, or particleboard.

• A Shoji screen with opaque rice-paper panels makes an oriental-style division that is decorative and practical.

• A fabric-covered screen can echo your decorating theme. For a tailored, urban look go for an upholstered screen finished with braid or close nailing.

95

mirrors

Mirrors reflect light, enhance the sense of space, and are essential for getting dressed. In an en-suite bath, a mirror can be used on a large scale to make the often confined space less claustrophobic. Mirrors can also add another decorative element—bamboo framed for the oriental look, rococo curves for the French boudoir, geometric for Art Deco style, beveled and etched for Venetian glamour.

get dressed

A tall, tilting mirror can stand anywhere convenient. There are reproduction antique styles and contemporary blond-wood-and-metal versions. A door-mounted mirror inside or outside a closet is practical if space is really tight, while the latest casual chic looks favor a huge mirror in a carved frame simply propped on the floor against the wall.

get made up

Position a makeup mirror so the natural light shines on your face. You may also need artificial lighting on either side. A triple mirror gives a good view, while a swivel mirror can be tilted.

96

picture perfect

A bedroom would be sterile without some pictures or decorative hangings. And remember, this is the room where you can indulge your taste without having to worry about what your visitors might think.

balance and proportion

Using pictures in a group will make a greater decorative impact than dotting them around the room in a haphazard manner. A large piece of furniture makes a good "anchor" for a group of pictures on the wall above, or a corner of the dressing table could be home to a gallery of small pictures. And if you have one large picture among small ones, put the large one at one end of the display.

There is something very soothing about a pair of symmetrically arranged pictures of equal size, perhaps one to either side of the bed or window. But there are times when a single picture—one fabulous work of art above the bed—has more impact than a group. And if your bedroom's small, don't think that a large picture or piece of artwork is out of the question; it can look stunning in a small space.

You must also consider the color of your walls. Pictures will have more "weight" if they are hung

against a block of color, and the darker the color, the more spectacular they will be. Heavily patterned wallpaper lessens the impact of pictures so if you also have a plain wall, hang the pictures there instead.

frames and mats

If you want impact, go for the heaviest, broadest frame you can find and a dramatic contrast between the style of the frame and the picture—for example, a battered antique gilded frame with a colorful modern painting.

Frames and mats can unify a disparate collection of pictures. Using matching—but not necessarily the same sized—frames and mats will bring a degree of harmony. Mats can also be used to make small pictures look more impressive. But bear in mind as well that if a picture's beautiful enough, it won't necessarily require any frame or mat.

to hang or not to hang?

Apart from the walls, where else can you display your pictures? A collection can be simply propped against a mantelpiece or even on the floor. Shelves offer another display space, or you might consider a single narrow, lipped shelf. This looks more interesting using pictures of various sizes and allowing some of them to overlap.

objects and ornaments

However delightfully decorated, a bedroom that doesn't reflect your personality is a sad place indeed. This is where all those objects you've collected over the years come in. Edit them judiciously and you can't go wrong.

the art of ornament

There is an art to display, so make your book collection more eye-catching in homemade paper covers in a single color or limited range of colors. And group objects according to a common element: all wooden items, ceramics, and so on.

arrangement matters

An arrangement on a wall has impact, so choose tall, freestanding shelving units or shelving you can "stack" into geometric shapes (see 86). Similarly, a large bulletin board with odds and ends pinned on it will have more impact than those same items dotted around the room.

Finally, give large, single objects added nighttime impact with an up- or downlight (see 56).

3

part three

keeping it fresh

what a refreshing experience! cleaning tips

It's so easy to let time go by without a thorough spring-cleaning, but it can be cathartic and will make a lot of difference to the presentation of your bedroom, so get that dust cloth out.

mattress

A mattress should be turned twice a year. Don't vacuum it, because that draws particles of skin and dust mite feces to the surface.

bed dressing

If you have any kind of bed draperies, dust will inevitably collect in the folds. If possible, wash them once a year; otherwise dry-clean or vacuum in situ, then take them down and shake them outside.

on the floor

Once a year, make sure you have carpeting and rugs professionally cleaned. They not only will look better but will last longer, too. If you have a hard floor, follow the manufacturer's advice for cleaning.

hidden horrors

It's amazing what you find when you look into and under things. Dust has a way of getting everywhere, so pull out drawers and completely empty your closets. And move the bed, too. Apart from making cleaning easier, this might just reveal that missing earring or shoe.

sweetly scented

When you have your annual or bi-annual clear-out, take the opportunity to keep your clothes smelling good with scented hanging sachets, and moth-free with pleasant-smelling cedarwood balls. Drawers can be refreshed with fragrant lining paper and scented sachets or soaps distributed among clothes, underwear, and towels.

make it over

99

When your bedroom starts looking a little tired but you're not ready for a complete change, making a few minor adjustments will add new zest.

giving windows a new look

Because window treatment styles can have such a profound effect on the look of a room, any changes you make to them will have instant impact. Try adding a deep contrasting border or sewing an unusual decorative trim along the front edge of curtains or draperies when you want a change.

changing seasons

A seasonal change of curtains or draperies provides both a refreshingly alternative look and an opportunity to have one set cleaned or repaired. And you could keep different sets of bedding: dark colors and heavy textures for winter, light neutral cottons and linens for summer.

cushions

Cushion covers are easy and inexpensive to make, so you can give cushions different seasonal looks, as you do for windows and bedding. Some new shapes will make all the difference, too.

cover story

Slipcovers aren't just for sofas; they work perfectly well for small, easy chairs, too. Envelope covers, held in place with fabric ties, are an easy-to-make alternative.

get a handle on it

Something as simple as changing the handles will update a tired chest of drawers or wardrobe. There are many interesting, amusing designs to suit any bedroom theme.

a lick of paint

Changing the color of a single wall will re-focus your bedroom style dramatically. If you picked the original color from a patterned fabric used in the room, choose a different color this time around. And if your bedroom doesn't have much pattern in it, you could add some colored stripes, circles, or squares while you're at it. Similarly, a coat or two of paint will transform tired old furniture.

exchange is no robbery

If a piece of furniture isn't fulfilling its function or doesn't really suit the look of the room; or if you've simply grown tired of it, then perhaps it should be banished or exchanged for something more serviceable and decorative.

100

flowers and plants

Flowers appeal to us with their beauty and sentimental associations, but above all, their scent is vital for a soothing bedroom environment.

take your pick

Bedroom flowers don't need to make a complex decorative statement. You can just use them in tiny, intimate arrangements for the bedside or dressing table, or try a scented flower head floating in a broad, flat bowl of water. It will perfume and re-hydrate your bedroom at the same time. A single highly perfumed lily or delicate orchid would be a good choice for the en-suite bath, which is often florally neglected, and remember that flowers can be used as a subtle means of echoing or contrasting with color accents in the bedroom.

seasons

Flowers are the natural witness to the seasons, and there is a special pleasure in choosing plants and flowers that genuinely reflect the time of year. Particularly in an urban environment, it's easy to lose sight of what's in flower, so reconnect with nature and choose your bedroom flowers with the season in mind.

avoiding allergies

There's an old tradition that flowers should be removed from the bedroom at night because they were considered unhealthful. Better to remove the pollen-bearing stamens where necessary to prevent allergic reactions and, where lilies are concerned, to prevent pollen stains.

flowers and herbs for aromatherapy

Aromas that comfort the mind and body are especially suitable for the bedroom. Think lavender, camomile, rosemary, and bergamot. Crush their leaves lightly to release the aromatic oils into the air.

Alternatively you might prefer pillows stuffed with dried flowers—the most popular is lavender—or essential-oil burners. Just don't leave them burning all night.

traditional flowers

Roses are a classic choice for a traditional bedroom, but choose only those that are rich in fragrance, rather than the perfect-bud but no-scent florist's alternatives!

modern flowers

For a minimalist bedroom, try an orchid or a single branch of cherry blossom in a spectacular container, perhaps placed in front of the window where the natural light will accentuate the shape, or lit from beneath against a textural or colored backdrop.

101

a change is as good as a rest

index

acknowledgments

Author's acknowledgments

To Jane O'Shea, thank you for giving me the opportunity to write this book. To Hilary Mandleberg, warmest gratitude for her endlessly good-natured guidance. To Paul Welti, thanks and admiration for his book layout. Finally, huge love to my husband, Francis, for patience, encouragement, and emergency cooking.

Picture credits

1 Ray Main/Mainstream; 2 centre Ray Main/Mainstream; 2 left Ray Main/Mainstream; 2 right Paul Massey/Mainstream; 3 centre Ray Main/Mainstream/Designers Collett-Zarzycki; 3 left Ray Main/Mainstream/Dev UsickHeal Associates; 3 right Ray Main/Mainstream/Arch Wells Mackereth; 4 below centre Ray Main/Mainstream; 4 above Ray Main/Mainstream/Design dalziel-pow; 4 above centre Ray Main/Mainstream; 7 Ray Main/Mainstream/Pearl Lowe; 8 Ray Main/ Mainstream/Architects McDowel&Benedetti; 9 Ray Main/Mainstream/Designers Collett-Zarzycki; 11 Ray Main/Mainstream; 12 Ray Main/Mainstream; 13 Ray Main/Mainstream; 14-15 Ray Main/Mainstream/Mulberry; 16-17 Darren Chung/Mainstream/Designer Emma Gower; 18-19 Ray Main/Mainstream/Developer Candy&Candy; 25 Ray Main/Mainstream/Architect Gregory Phillips; 26-27 Ray Main/Mainstream/ Developer Candy&Candy; 29 Ray Main/Mainstream; 30-31 Ray Main/Mainstream/Pearl Lowe; 31 Ray Main/Mainstream; 32 Ray Main/Mainstream; 33 Ray Main/Mainstream/Peter Wadley Architects; 34-35 Ray Main/Mainstream; 37 Ray Main/Mainstream/Developer Sapcote Lofts; 38-39 Ray Main/Mainstream/Chateau De Massillan; 40-41 Ray Main/Mainstream; 43 Ray Main/Mainstream; 44-45 Ray Main/Mainstream/Architect Spencer Fung; 45 Ray Main/Mainstream; 46-7 Ray Main/Mainstream/Mathmos; 47 Ray Main/Mainstream; 48 Ray Main/Mainstream; 49 Ray Main/Mainstream; 51 below left Ray Main/Mainstream; 51 above right Ray Main/Mainstream/London & Country Homes; 51 below right Darren Chung/Mainstream/Linda Barker/Laura Ashley; 51 above left Ray Main/Mainstream; 52-3 below Ray Main/Mainstream/ Patel Taylor Architects; 52-3 above Ray Main/Mainstream; 54-5 above Ray Main/Mainstream; 54-55 below Ray Main/Mainstream/Designer Claire Nash: 57 above left Ray Main/Mainstream; 57 above right Ray Main/Mainstream; 57 below left Ray Main/Mainstream; 57 below right Ray Main/Mainstream; 58 inset Ray Main/Mainstream/LTS Architects; 58 main Ray Main/Mainstream Designer Missher Crossland; 59 Ray Main/Mainstream; 61 Ray Main/Mainstream; 62-3 Ray Main/Mainstream/Designer Sasha Wadell; 64-5 Ray Main/Mainstream; 66-67 Ray Main/Mainstream/Architect John Pawson; 68-69 Ray Main/Mainstream; 70 Ray Main/Mainstream/Pearl Lowe; 71 Ray Main/Mainstream/Designer Nick Allen; 72-73 Ray Main/Mainstream/Architect Sabrina Foster; 73 Ray Main/Mainstream/Designer Roger Oates; 74 below Ray Main/Mainstream; 74 centre Ray Main/Mainstream; 74 above Ray Main/Mainstream/Designer Jo Warman; 74-75 Ray Main/Mainstream; 77 Paul Massey/Mainstream; 78-9 Darren Chung/Mainstream; 80 Ray Main/Mainstream/Developer Sapcote Lofts; 80-81 Ray Main/Mainstream; 82-83 Ray Main/Mainstream/Designer L.Llewelyn-Bowen; 85 Ray Main/Mainstream/Barratta Design; 86 Ray Main/Mainstream/Mark Guard Architects; 87 Ray Main/Mainstream/www.w2products.com; 88-89 Colefax & Fowler/ Jane Churchill for Larkfield Leaf wallpaper; 88-89 Lewis & Wood for Elizabeth wallpaper; 91 Ray Main/ Mainstream/Architect Featherstone; 92 left Ray Main/Mainstream; 92 right Ray Main/Mainstream; 93 Ray Main/Mainstream; 94 Ray Main/Mainstream; 95 Ray Main/Mainstream; 97 Ray Main/Mainstream/The Rookery; 98-99 Ray Main/Mainstream/Plain & Simple Kitchens; 100-1 Ray Main/Mainstream; 102 Darren Chung/Mainstream; 103 Ray Main/Mainstream; 104 Ray Main/Mainstream/ Developer Candy&Candy; 104-5 above Paul Massey/Mainstream; 104-5 below Ray Main/Mainstream/Designer William Yeoward; 106 Ray Main/Mainstream; 106-107 Ray Main/Mainstream/MMR Architects; 108 Ray Main/Mainstream/Chateau De Massillan; 109 Ray Main/Mainstream; 110 Ray Main/Mainstream; 110-111 Ray Main/Mainstream/ Designer Vincente Wolfe; 113 Ray Main/Mainstream/ Designer claire Nash; 114 Paul Massey/Mainstream/Architect John Pawson; 115 Ray Main/Mainstream/Developer Candy&Candy; 116 Ray Main/Mainstream/John Minshaw Designs; 117 Ray Main/Mainstream